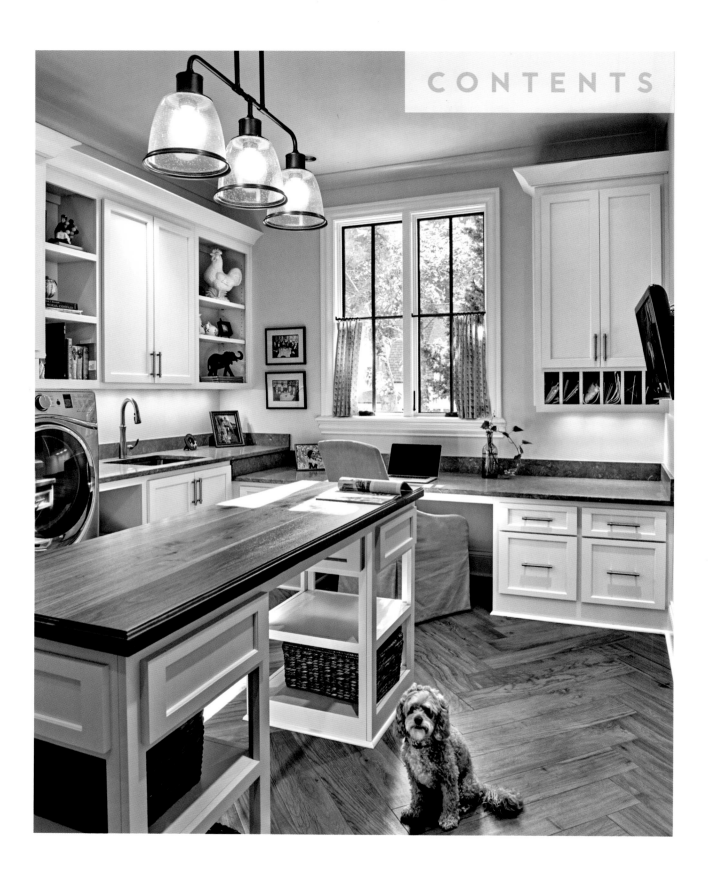

GREAT HOMES POSSESS A SPIRIT THAT TRANSCENDS THEIR PARTS

In a purely physical sense, a house is little more than a collection of thousands of parts assembled over six months or more to provide shelter. But to the people who live there, it is much more—it's a canvas, an intimate reflection of our lifestyle, tastes, and aspirations. It mirrors our priorities, whether they are collecting Eames furniture, breeding roses, enjoying happy hours next to a fire pit, or owning an architectural masterpiece that's the envy of the neighborhood. When a house aligns with our personal goals and enriches our lives, we live in a great home.

The intriguing question is how design empowers that perception. The starting point would be an ideal layout that facilitates options as simple as monitoring your children playing, or as complex as creating an ideal spot for a heightened yoga experience. It doesn't take much for some people to feel like they live in a great home. A killer back porch at the edge of the woods—a place to sip coffee on a cool morning, spot birds, or play bluegrass music with friends—may be all that's needed. For some people, bricks, sticks, and mortar may be immaterial. They may simply prize the connection to neighbors and community. Surveys show that homebuyers search for a tree-lined block, an award-winning school district, or an ideal new-home community before they settle on a particular house.

When it comes to the delights of architecture, some homes simply resonate more deeply than others. Ask most architects to describe a great home, and they invariably point to proportions—alignments between the roof surfaces, window size, and home height. Or they may talk about how the building was designed "correctly," with appropriate details for its style, or the way it relates to its environment. It's high praise when architects or builders say they would like to live in a particular house, since they are in the business of creating them.

What's particularly interesting is that the same homes rise to the top of multiple design competitions each year. It's as if the industry shared an archetypal vision of successful design. I've always thought that, if the factors that shape that perception could be put into words and identified with images, maybe the quality of new homes built each year could be elevated. Because—let's face it—many new homes do not improve the aesthetics of the built environment.

Yet typically there is agreement about award-winning homes, whether modern, traditional, or something in between. Their appearance is modest and creative, rather than tacky or forced. Their bones shine through, revealing how they were built, in an intelligent fashion. More often than not, the best homes embrace state-of-the art technology to reduce operating costs and improve homeowner controls, often rendering those controls invisible. Their flexible floor plans can be adapted as life circumstances shift. To win an award, whether it's from the American Institute of Architects, a home builder association, or a shelter magazine, architectural details need to be interpreted, designed, and built correctly. And interiors must deliver on the promise of the exteriors—a critical failing of much mass-market housing.

The funny thing is that the best homes often produce an emotional response—you know immediately whether you like them or not, just as you do when you meet a sympathetic stranger. You are drawn by the way they look from the street. Then, as you walk their rooms and halls and porches, you start to imagine living in them. You visualize spending an evening with your family at home—you are making street tacos while your teenager sits at the kitchen island slaving over biology homework. You imagine having friends visit, sharing drinks and stories beside a backyard fire pit. You think about escaping to a private room to read a British murder novel or doing morning stretches in your Zen garden.

Lately I've been doubling back with architects who routinely win architectural competitions to get their ideas on what results in a great home. My goal in picking their brains and analyzing their projects is to develop a package of core design principles. So many books and websites express these ideas in a technical fashion—in so-called architect-speak. I've tried to present my discoveries in a way that everyone can understand. Even if you can't afford to hire an elite architect to design your home, you could employ these principles to improve your life at home.

Rooms, for example, feel more inviting with windows on at least two sides to promote cross breezes. Having a room away from the family room where you can practice trumpet, draw, or write may be vital to your mental well-being, especially if the public rooms are wide open. Having a thoughtfully laid out kitchen, so that you don't have to run a track meet to cook a meal, can be a godsend. Homebuyer surveys show that having enough storage to declutter a house is critically important to satisfaction. You may really come to appreciate a mudroom by the back door for shedding backpacks, suitcases, and dirty shoes.

At industry meetings, architects often reference the same iconic homes as the greatest achievements. What is it about Frank Lloyd Wright's Fallingwater, Jefferson's Monticello, the classic Sears Bungalow, or the Case Study Houses commissioned by *Arts + Architecture* magazine that people love so much? A big part of the attraction is a strong architectural aesthetic, one that raises the design to the realm of art. Interestingly, the most cherished homes usually also work on a practical level. They often harness the power of the sun, present great views of the natural landscape, and execute interior details true to their style. They have a strong personality, one that reflects the character of an ingenious designer, conscientious builder, or impassioned owner.

Great design lies within everyone's reach, and that's a good thing. In all but the darkest times, we aspire to live in a better environment. That's true of the homeless who upgrade from newspaper to cardboard on a park bench, or the corporate executive who trades from a brownstone in the Bronx to a swank apartment in Manhattan. Indeed, to many people, a home is great simply because they have one, especially if they worked long and hard to buy it. But as this book attempts to demonstrate, it can also be the starting point for even greater satisfaction, personal growth, and enjoyment.

1.
CHARACTERISTICS
OF A
GREAT HOME

ICONIC HOMES SHARE COMMON ELEMENTS OF STYLE AND SUBSTANCE

As a shelter magazine editor for more than twenty years, I routinely gathered leading architects and builders to bestow awards on the best homes built in the last year. We would present the jury with criteria: Does the home connect to its environment? It couldn't stick out like a skyscraper on a street of ranches or be a menacing outsider in an otherwise unspoiled natural landscape. Was it built with materials appropriate to its style? There's something special about South Texas homes designed with native, creamy-white limestone, urban townhomes framed with exposed steel beams, and New England cottages clad with board and batten siding. Maybe most important, did the design meet the needs of its owners, whether Silicon Valley executives, the mythical statistical family with 1.5 children, or even low-income renters?

The judges would soak up the direction, then go their own way. They invariably hunted out the most architecturally compelling projects, rewarding homes that made fresh statements, and architects and builders who successfully experimented with the next big thing. That could be building to the highest sustainability standard, or just designing a great looking, affordable production home. They consistently rewarded clean, honest design that did more with less, even during the housing boom when Americans built the biggest homes possible to ride the raging wave of equity gains. The best-looking new home—whether an adobe retreat in the desert, a shingled cottage by the sea, or a gritty loft in the city—was the least pretentious. All design competitions draw excessive homes with unlimited budgets. They rarely win.

Each year our juries selected a home of the year. One year the recipient was an unpretentious, 1,800-square-foot West-Indies-inspired vacation home in Rosemary Beach, Florida. With its quirky floor plan and an exterior ready to take on the fiercest squall, the home provoked an immediate emotional appeal. The judges decided they "just loved it." Their ardor started with the rickety, weather-beaten fence facing the street, which turned out to be a construction barrier that Darrell Russell of A Boheme Design, the architect who initially lived in the home, was later forced to remove. One judge said he liked the way the fence mimicked the rhythm of the porch balusters. Another commented on how the home appeared anchored to the ground, an impression owing from a firm concrete foundation and sturdy columns that rose from the sand to support the roof. Deep roof overhangs covered porches to ensure an enjoyable day at the beach, no matter how rainy or sunny.

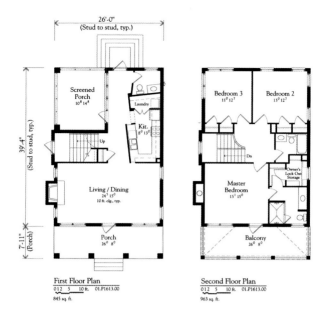

26'-0"
(Stud to stud, typ.)

39'-4"
(Stud to stud, typ.)

7'-11"
(Porch)

Screened Porch
10⁸ 14⁸

Laundry

Kit.
8⁰ 13⁰

Up

Living / Dining
24⁵ 15⁰
10 ft. clg., typ.

Porch
26⁰ 8⁰

First Floor Plan
0 1 2   5   10 ft.   01.P1613.00
845 sq. ft.

Bedroom 3
11⁰ 12⁷

Bedroom 2
13⁰ 12⁷

Master Bedroom
13¹ 15⁰

Dn

Owner's Lock Out Storage

Balcony
26⁰ 8⁰

Second Floor Plan
0 1 2   5   10 ft.   01.P1613.00
963 sq. ft.

Anchored in the sand, with a strong metal roof and sheltering eaves, the Rosemary Beach House is ready to take on the hot sun and foul weather. *Photo by Jeffrey Jacobs*

PLANS / An angled wall adds a quirky element to the foursquare plan.

After the jury made its decision, we discovered that a variation on the home design had won the competition several years before, when someone else was editing the magazine. It turned out that Russell had built the plan in reverse for a previous home in Memphis. He added porches to the front façade of the Rosemary Beach house and reorganized some rooms inside, moving public rooms to the front. The two homes were different enough that two awards seemed deserved. Still, the situation raised an intriguing question: how could the same basic design rise to the top of two different competitions, each with more than 500 entries, each with a unique set of six judges? Something about the design struck a very fundamental chord.

A big part of the attraction, at least the second time around, was the way the interiors reinforced the down-home promise made by the front façade. Few judges had seen this done on a Cracker house, a regional and quite practical style that grew out of working housing in the coastal southeast. Russell, an interior designer as well as an architect, covered walls in the kitchen, bath, and upstairs hallway with corrugated metal. He blanketed other interior walls with the same stained flush boards that clad the exterior. He literally brought the outside in by using broken limestone, seashells, and crab casings to create a floor mosaic in the second-story hallway.

Juries in design competitions invariably praise restraint, another quality the simple Rosemary Beach home imbued. The best homes, even the biggest mansions, don't throw on dormers, stone, or molding in ways that aren't authentic. Porches, shutters, and drainpipes serve a purpose first, their beauty often derived from the way they do their work. Russell left shutters off the Rosemary Beach house because hurricane-resistant windows render them superfluous. With a big two-story porch dominating the exterior, it didn't make sense to doll up the stucco walls either. A few simple porch lights sufficed.

Great homes come in all styles and forms. The competitions we ran drew winners from dramatically different worlds. Some homes won for fresh takes on traditional Old World styles. Every year, it seemed, we'd have a stunning shingle-style winner from a Northeastern beach location with whimsical nautical elements, such as a widow's walk or a bell

tower. Contemporary homes with horizontal wood siding, flat roofs, and warm wood interiors were a favorite. We also awarded our share of modern designs, homes that made heavy use of metal and glass with exquisite indoor-outdoor relationships, the same style of home that monopolizes high-end architectural competitions.

Regardless of the style, we insisted that plans still work for the homeowner. The roof, no matter how interesting, couldn't direct rainwater to the head of visitors standing outside the front door. The maintenance requirements of cedar-clad beach houses couldn't monopolize summer vacations. An open stairwell shouldn't be an open invitation to the emergency room at the children's hospital. Sometimes you'd wonder, looking at the lack of handrails and side walls in some stair entries, whether building inspectors were blindfolded at the door. The reality is that architects often design two stairways—one that meets codes for the building inspector, and a more stylish one for award submissions.

The worst modern homes blatantly disregard privacy in stubborn pursuit of the ultimate landscaped view. Their walls of big windows may severely compromise long-term operating costs and cause glare. Architectural whimsy, like the escape hatch an architect included in one of Brad Pitt's Lower Ninth demonstration homes in New Orleans after Hurricane Katrina, just in case it were to float away, is sometimes better described as folly. In the worst case, scant attention to weatherproofing "imaginative" details may spell financial ruin for homeowners, wiping out their most important long-term source of equity.

Judges consistently praise the honest use of natural, indigenous materials, especially when combined in innovative ways. They often award homes that do a particularly good job responding to the natural environment—the way windows bathe interior walls with sunlight. Envy sometimes creeps into the competition, and you hear a judge mutter under his or her breath, "Gee, I wish I had designed that." One year a judge was so impressed with a townhome design he'd seen the day before—the plan staggered the depth of homes to produce private back decks and front stoops—something you see in urban neighborhoods built more than a hundred years ago—that we caught him at breakfast the next morning sketching it for a fellow jurist who wanted to build it.

Another home of the year stood out for its compact form and expressive material use. After looking at a series of luxury houses tricked out with over-the-top drywall details, bizarre lighting, and big, poorly conceived rooms, the judges gave the top award to an unpretentious 1,400-square-foot home designed by Obie G. Bowman Architect. A fabulous location, atop a bluff overlooking the ocean in Point Arena, California, made the home expensive to build. But one judge was so taken with the home, especially the interior details and exterior decking, that he paid it the ultimate compliment—"It looks like a great house to live in."

Little did the judges know that the Clark house was the result of several major mid-stream compromises between architect, homeowner, and contractor. Bowman had finished two conceptual drawings when the homeowner threw him a curve: she wanted a wrap-around porch on at least two sides to capitalize on ocean views and breezes. The porch

FLOOR PLAN

0   5   10   15

In this small, two-bedroom house, rooms borrow light and views from each other. A bright pine log in the hall contrasts with warm Douglas fir in the ceiling. *Photo courtesy Obie G. Bowman Architect*

The entry vestibule does double duty as a cultural center with a piano and rolling library shelves. *Photo courtesy Obie G. Bowman Architect*

PLANS / The plan separates public from private spaces, an especially important consideration in small homes. *Diagram courtesy Obie G. Bowman Architect*

overhangs would block precious natural light from entering the home. Bowman was already concerned about light reaching living spaces because the lot was surrounded by trees and enshrouded with heavy fog many days of the year. "Point Arena is probably one of the foggiest places on earth," he says.

The request forced Bowman to rethink how to light the interior spaces. He wound up designing a large central skylight in the hipped roof. Installing the skylight was no simple chore—it had to be lowered in place with a crane. But the result was fantastic. "We designed a pyramidal shape at the top of the roof with a skylight system that brings light into every room," he says. "We added clerestory windows between rooms that allow light to pass into every space. The client's request led to a solution that I wouldn't have come up with otherwise. The house was much better as a result."

Bowman focused on a few memorable details on the front of the house—a five-by-ten-foot commercial door, capped by a gutter carved into a large redwood beam. The home's small footprint forced him to make some rooms do double-duty. One wall of the entry vestibule serves as a cultural center with an upright piano and floor-to-ceiling bookshelves accessed from a rolling ladder.

The architect's willingness to compromise stands in contrast to the operating philosophy of many renowned architects, who want to ensure that their vision is the one built. Bowman's teacher, the legendary architect Charles Moore, told architectural students to keep an open mind about client desires and outside suggestions. "He said, 'Don't have preconceived notions about the design. It's a mistake to say that you can't deviate,'" says Bowman. "I like to accept new ideas. Mrs. Clark wanted a wrap-around porch. I had to find a solution. There are always solutions." He adds jokingly, "but you probably don't get a Richard Meier building that way."

The division of private and public spaces within the Clark house is another common denominator to great home design. Separate zones become especially important in large open plans with easy sound transfer. Putting the baby to bed is problematic with the latest Tom Cruise movie running on a home theater system in a cavernous family room below. Similarly, great room plans need some kind of away space, a retreat where family members who don't want to watch the latest action adventure can stretch their mind or body. Flexible great room plans, for all the glorious living space they provide, create a corresponding need to escape.

The best homes succeed on both architectural and practical levels, and there's no reason why they shouldn't deliver on both. The best modern homes, even ones with austere, clean interiors, still provide storage space, though it's often concealed. A master bathroom that borders on being a spa can't overlook the need for convenient storage of medicine bottles, bulky hair dryers, and messy toothpaste. Kitchens may be masterpieces of industrial design, but they can't disregard the dirty work that gets done there. Front entries need to make a strong first impression. But are a twenty-foot ceiling and a $5,000 chandelier really necessary when visitors are more likely to look through the space to a landscaped courtyard or backyard?

THE BEST HOMES INVARIABLY WORK OVERTIME TO CAPTURE EXTERIOR VIEWS—some even seem subservient
to this noble purpose. The ones that win major architectural awards often have the built-in advantage of extraordinary
natural surroundings—ocean or lake views, mountaintops, or dense forests. But those sites present their share of
challenges as well. That was the case with the Stonington House, designed by Jim Estes of Estes Twombly Architects on
seven acres that rim the Atlantic Ocean. Protected wetlands to the east and west left a small piece of land on which to
build. Natural surroundings made the orientation of the home and garden especially important.

Complicating the situation was Estes's perennial desire to make the most of solar heating and passive cooling. New
Englanders crave the warmth of winter sunlight as they achingly wait for spring. A century ago, Yankees intuitively
designed farm buildings that extended the warm seasons and provided natural ventilation during the summer. An avid
bicyclist, Estes loves to study details in the old agriculture buildings that dot the countryside. He is convinced that the
best buildings are never published in magazines for professionals to study. Locals who drive by in cars may not even
fully appreciate them. "The best thing about taking a bike is that you can stop and look around," he says.

Estes separated the Stonington House from the wetlands with a wall of local granite that encloses sheltered courtyards
and a small manicured lawn. "The best architectural solutions," Estes says, "appear almost inevitable after applying the
logic of the site."

In the main house, big public rooms face a wall of south-facing glass that heats space in the winter when the sun is low in the sky. A porch overhang blocks harsh light on summer days when the sun is high. The Stonington House, like most of Estes's designs, is purposely narrow, only one room wide, so that ocean breezes can cool it. Cool air enters through low windows on one side, exiting through high windows on the other. Transoms circulate light and air through the few enclosed rooms in the house.

A large exterior stone wall—the same material used to form the fireplace inside—speaks to the region's craftsman tradition. Yet Estes insists on letting the bones of the structure—roof beams, poles, and trusses—shine through on the interior. He goes so far as to insulate the roof on the exterior so that he can leave structural elements exposed inside. His heavy use of glass and metal to break down walls between the inside and outside is unmistakably modern.

Even so, it's clear that Estes draws inspiration from the honest utilitarianism of agricultural buildings. His buildings appear designed to get work done—shed snow, stand up to ocean breezes, and last for generations— rather than impress neighbors. That philosophy sometimes gets tested when the client wants a large, showy kitchen. The size of the kitchen "is always a conversation," allows the architect, who admits that his kitchen designs have grown more elaborate in recent years.

2.
MAKE A PERSONAL STATEMENT

THE BEST HOMES REFLECT THEIR OWNERS' PERSONALITIES

The best homes ultimately reflect their owners' personality, even when architects leave their imprint. Some designers are better than others at accepting this fact of human nature. To them, a new home isn't complete until a family moves in, spreads out, and marks the space. The infamous Charles Moore once wrote that great architecture celebrates the fact that occupancy brings enhancement and completion. Humans, he believed, have a basic drive to manipulate interior spaces and distinguish them from the outside, an urge that architects should assist rather than thwart, even if it conflicts with the interior scheme. One of the masters of personalization is Jefferson Riley of Centerbrook Architects and Planners, one of several firms that Moore founded. One year Riley spoke about his design philosophy to leading architects and builders gathered to celebrate an anniversary celebration of our magazine's awards program. He began by saying that his work was deeply influenced not by an architectural mentor, but by a place—a fourteen-cabin family camp in the north woods of Maine that his grandfather built at the turn of the century. It was here that Riley spent his most memorable summers as a kid. The architect's viewpoint was also informed by two vocations that still bring him joy. Before becoming an architect, he mastered the art of building wood boats. And while studying sculpture in France, he sketched people in parks and bistros.

Before designing a home, Riley digs to discover what brings joy to the hearts of his clients. He sketches design details that speak to these experiences, memories, and talents. Great homes, he believes, evoke memories of special places where you've lived and visited. They may even tell stories about them. Great homes, for that reason, are often nostalgic, incorporating pieces of imagination and history. Judges flipping through page after page of entry brochures would stop cold at the unusual, inspired details in Riley's homes—a nautilus-shaped balustrade, a kitchen wall that held a rusted metal hand-tool collection, a fireplace mantel with mementos from an African trip.

Jefferson Riley's Beside the Point remarries a historic façade to the streetscape, hiding a large addition in back. *Photo by Robert Benson*

A collection of arcane hand tools highlights a kitchen. White cabinets mimic a pattern from antique vented cupboards. *Photo by Robert Benson*

The hull of a wooden boat graces the ceiling of the master bedroom, a personal touch for owners who love to sail. *Photo by Robert Benson*

ONE YEAR CENTERBROOK WON FOR BESIDE THE POINT, the remodel of a nineteenth-century river home that had lost its identity through a series of insensitive "remuddlings." Riley managed to personalize the home even as he accomplished a complex historic renovation. He found space above sliding patio doors in the kitchen to exhibit the owner's collection of old hand tools. Wider-than-normal hallways on the first and second floors showcase an art collection. Because the owners love to sail, Riley designed a boat form into the master bedroom ceiling. Wrapped in clapboard, it looks like the hull of a wooden boat—a keel hides air diffusers. He also made sure that virtually every room offers a river view.

Homeowners invariably take on remodeling projects to add additional living space, an objective that complicates a historic renovation. Step one is to determine what can actually be preserved. A forensic examination revealed that the home's original timber frame and rubble foundation was so far gone it would need to be rebuilt. Riley drew up plans to meticulously restore the front façade, remarrying it to a street of old colonial homes in an historic district. He gained permission to add a new garage on the front side by tucking it into the hillside away from the main house. The garage, along with a natural rock outcropping, defines a new entry courtyard. A sizable addition to the rear of the home, facing the river, can't be seen from the street.

Riley's personal approach stands in contrast to the method that some architects bring to the table. They may listen to a client's needs for bedroom and bathroom count and preferred living spaces. They may carefully consider limitations or opportunities posed by the site. But then, as Riley pointed out in his presentation, they dig in to design the home they are most interested in drawing, one that meets a pre-determined agenda or dogma, one that they expect to get published and further their reputation. Problems arise when the architect's vision collides with the homeowner's agenda, especially if the home goes over budget due to the designer's prized details.

But as any architect would point out, this is a balancing act. People hire an architect because they want a special home, one imbued with a certain aesthetic. Most homeowners meet with several architects before they hire one whose design and personality is the best match. For example, a graphic artist friend interviewed a short list of architects to design her home several years ago. After indulging the many creative ideas that my friend had for her house—she wanted a cork kitchen floor and concrete countertops, and she had picked out bathroom tile by a local artist—the architect said, "You know, what you will get is my design." She decided to go with another architect who was more willing to accept her ideas.

Local masons and artisans, working
from House + House's drawings,
produced virtually all the home's
details by hand, including the
expressive stair rail. *Photo courtesy
House + House Architects*

A thick art ledge in the brightly lit
living room recalls the heavy street
wall. *Photo courtesy House + House
Architects*

ARCHITECTS DESIGN SOME OF THE GREATEST HOMES FOR THEIR OWN USE, a business arrangement that certainly makes it easier to meet the client's needs. It also provides creative license to attempt something special. That was the case with architects Steven and Cathi House's renovation of their home high in the mountains of San Miguel de Allende, Mexico. The inspiring, forward-looking project achieved a kind of legendary status in residential architecture circles. Built in 1995, it presaged trends that drive the best residential design even today. The Houses, who live in San Francisco but whose firm, House + House Architects, does a lot of work in Mexico, stumbled upon a crumbling old house during a search for stone in San Miguel, a 460-year-old Spanish colonial town protected as a UNESCO World Heritage site. The center for art and culture, replete with ancient churches, cobblestone streets, and crumbing walls draped in bougainvillea, has become a mecca for many highly skilled and creative craftspeople.

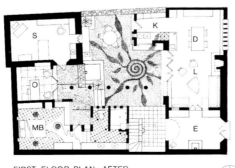

FIRST FLOOR PLAN · AFTER

SECOND FLOOR PLAN · AFTER

The structure that caught the House's attention was little more than a weathered door in a crumbling stucco wall, hardly noticeable from the street. The door opened to an abandoned hacienda with dilapidated rooms that had been divided through the years among children and grandchildren. The "little ruin" captured their hearts, igniting a fantasy about having a retreat in an exotic land. It wasn't long before some practical concerns brought them down to earth.

"All indications were that it would probably be a nightmare to build in Mexico," recalls Steven. Strict building codes protect the city's built heritage, and the Houses weren't that familiar with local building practices. As the couple explored the feasibility of building in San Miguel de Allende, they discovered an alternative universe of local artisans and craftsman. They quickly became inspired by the possibility of working hand in glove with them. "We decided to celebrate every material, process, and hand that touched any part of our home. We used only local materials and details, and decided that our home would be made without power tools," Steven says.

The 2,000-square-foot home the Houses designed is a little village of sorts with interweaving rooms, stairways, balconies, and roof terraces. A sunny central courtyard, the element that captured the imagination of their peers, organizes the otherwise disparate spaces. It reads like a complete outdoor room with furniture, a fireplace, and native plants. It serves as a central cooling system, circulating air through major rooms of the house and is effective enough that the Houses dispensed with mechanical heating and cooling. Two fireplaces provide back-up heat for cold mountain nights.

The home's green agenda was extreme even by today's standards. Everything worth preserving from the original buildings was recycled into new uses. The effort started with restoring the weather-beaten door that caught their fancy. The adobe wall along the street was retouched and reinforced to carry a new roof and second floor. A storage shed was refurbished into a studio. Stone paving was re-cut and reused. Brick floors in the living room and studio were refinished. Roof tiles were reclaimed from collapsed buildings. Multi-colored stone originally used for paths was repurposed to build the stairway and steps that wrap the courtyard.

Working without material catalogs or the help of a local lumberyard, the Houses illustrated virtually every architectural detail, including the windows and doors. They designed steel railings, hinges, hardware, and furniture, all of it forged and hammered into shapes from raw steel. Local tradition influenced the design of brick railings and a "boveda" ceiling. Black cantera stone, another local staple, was cut by hand into columns and rain and fountain spouts. An existing stone wall was doubled in height in the same random pattern.

Some highly personal touches remind the Houses of prior home projects or earlier stages of their lives. Stone from previous homes was set into the colored concrete kitchen counters. A stone pattern in the courtyard—done with black slate from nearby mountains combined with ochre-colored stones collected from a dry riverbed just outside of town—tells a story from their life. Ancient carvings placed throughout the house reference the region's past. The details combine to form a meaningful and idiosyncratic home.

ON MOST PROJECTS, OF COURSE, ARCHITECTS MUST INTERVIEW CLIENTS TO GET A WISH LIST. Johnsen Schmaling Architects begins each commission with a long interview. The firm wants to know how the clients currently live at home, and how they would want to live in a new home. Do they watch television in the living room, family room, or bedroom? Where do they entertain guests—in the kitchen or living room? Do they celebrate holidays with formal meals in the dining room? How often do guests actually stay the night? How much and what kind of work do they do at home? The answers inform a personalized design program.

"We try to get the narrative of their lives," says Sebastian Schmaling. "People may never eat at home, so they don't need a dining room or a large kitchen. They may want an observatory more than they want a space to entertain guests. Everyone says they want a den and a guest bedroom, but they may only have guests two days a year, so

The Redaction House by Johnsen Schmaling Architects, a home for a visual artist, unmercifully filters out views of prosaic neighboring houses. *Photo by John J. Macaulay/ Johnsen Schmaling Architects*

why not create a den that could be converted to a guest bedroom when you need it? Things are bad when preconceptions rule."

Clients start on the wrong foot when they come to Schmaling with specifications to maximize a return on their land investment. Brokers may convince them that a 3,500-square-foot house requires four bedrooms and three and a half baths to retain resale value. "That doesn't mean anything. The house could still feel tight," Schmaling says. "There's dumb and smart square footage. You can make rooms a third smaller if you borrow space from other rooms via sight lines, adjacencies, and views to the outside. Quality matters more than quantity. Fifteen years ago people complained about their plate not being filled at the restaurant. Today they understand that good food has nothing to do with a lot of food. People who want to live in an architect-design house understand that concept."

Schmaling's interview process often results in a deeply personalized, unique home, like the one he designed on a lake in suburban Wisconsin for a fiber artist and her young family. Deliberately introverted, the Redaction House focuses attention on the water, filtering out views of large, prosaic homes that circle the lake. Architects often design homes that edit out views of power lines, alleys, and other eyesores. Schmaling took the same approach to the dull production homes that circle the lake. "The home functions as an optic filter," he says.

The 2,900-square-foot house—it resembles a two-story wood cube—is built on a narrow sliver of land previously considered too small for new construction. Zoning restrictions prohibited traditional design approaches. Schmaling's solution was to cut into the sloping ground to create a pad for a stepped brick podium. The move produced a main floor that feels suspended in a tree canopy, and a walkout basement with room for two bedrooms and a family room. Walkout basements are so desirable that some developers grade otherwise flat ground to create lots that can support them.

The process of visual redaction begins with a narrow path that leads from the street into a long, straight entry courtyard surrounded by a slotted brick wall. Perforations decrease as you draw closer to the house, creating the sense that you are being drawn into shelter, or perhaps focusing a lens. Once you reach the house, a glass door frames an unencumbered view of the lake, leaving out most of the surrounding homes. "It's like a viewfinder on your camera," he says. "You have to continue to experience the home before you get a bigger view."

Once inside, visitors look diagonally across wide-open living space (a perspective that makes the space appear larger) to a two-story wall of stacked "apertures." A series of windows and wall panels once again focuses attention only on desirable views of the lake, sky, and trees. Before construction begins, Schmaling visualizes what it would be like to sit and stand in nearly every interior space. To preserve views, he groups most rooms along the perimeter of a central gathering space. A tall fireplace wall with glass on either side visually divides the great room from a large glass-walled deck.

A foundation of Illinois brick supports the stacked rectangular forms, though many of its corners either disappear (thanks to butted glass) or are missing (due to cantilevers). Recessed windows and doors add to the perception. Red, blue, yellow, and green vertical slats reference the polychrome threads the fiber artist uses in her work. They playfully contrast with dark-stained horizontal cedar siding sourced from Northern Wisconsin. A three-quarter-inch air gap between the cladding and the building envelope creates a rain screen to prevent moisture buildup, an essential detail if the building is going to stand up to its harsh northern climate.

A long, diagonal view from the entry makes the home read much larger than its footprint. *Photo by John J. Macaulay/Johnsen Schmaling Architects*

3.
HARMONIZE
WITH NATURE

THE BEST HOMES SERVE AS A PORTAL TO THEIR NATURAL SURROUNDINGS

When Jim Cutler interviewed for the job of designing their home, the Newbergs took him to a spot at the top of a pristine hill, their first choice for locating the retreat. As Cutler stood there, reflecting on the long driveway that would have to cut through a forested hillside, a flash of light caught his eye—a reflection from a small pond at the bottom of the hill. "What's that?" he asked, pointing in the direction of the water. "An old logger's pond that's about ninety percent filled in," the clients replied. After an inspection revealed that the pond could be easily dredged, Cutler convinced the Newbergs that the pond might be a better place to build their house.

The Newberg residence ultimately straddled the cleaned out and expanded pond. At only 1,440 square feet with a separate 550-square-foot guesthouse, the home speaks volumes about the special relationship between homes and their natural surroundings. The most important element of a great home may be the way it relates to hills, fields, lakes, and other natural elements, features that are likely to last much longer than the home built near them. The best homes acknowledge their temporal status.

Cutler's design puts recreation at the home's doorstep—children of all ages can dive into the pond from the deck. Or else they can sit on deck chairs and admire the wild creatures that regularly or occasionally visit. Visitors who approach from the parking lot, 150 feet removed from the main house, would never know what's in store. In a carefully orchestrated sequence, they walk single-file down a crushed-stone path, purposely narrowed by forest trees and giant rhododendrons, to a bridge where the house finally comes into view.

For all its openness in back, the front of the house, little more than a series of wide vertical planks topped by clerestory windows, protects the Newburgs' privacy. The pond only becomes visible when the front door opens; it's guaranteed to be a memorable experience. "The pond feels four times bigger when you approach it through a constricted path and see it when you open the door," says Cutler, of Cutler Anderson Architects. "It's like seeing the moon on the horizon. It's seems bigger there than when it's high in the sky."

The house works for children of all ages. *Photo courtesy of Cutler Anderson Architects*

Cutler devotes most of his energy and budget to rooms occupied the most. Weight-balanced patio doors slide up with the push of a finger and stay in place. *Photo courtesy of Cutler Anderson Architects*

Beams in the ceiling appear to pierce the wall and connect with rafters outside. *Photo courtesy of Cutler Anderson Architects.*

Visitors travel a narrow, tree-lined path that ultimately opens to views of the home. High clerestory windows preserve the Newbergs' privacy while channeling light to the interior. *Photo courtesy of Cutler Anderson Architects*

Cutler's formula is to economize on the building form, saving money for exquisite interior details in key spots. The Newburg house, true to form, is a simple rectangular box, a shape that provides the most living space for the dollar. Cutler economized on less frequently used rooms such as the garage and bedrooms, built slab-on-grade, with trusses and standard walls and trim details. He devoted money and energy to details in the great room and kitchen, the rooms where the family hangs out the most. The center of attention are large vertical lift doors that are easy to raise, thanks to fifteen-pound lead counterweights. There's enough friction in the system to keep the doors in an upright position.

Cutler designed the lift doors along with all the hardware and lighting in the home. No bolt is left unconsidered. No joint left to chance. And it's all revealed. Cutler may draw as many as 300 details for a project, including lowly bolts, cabinet hardware, and door knobs. He wants to make sure that the material is properly respected, its nature revealed. "I was ruined when I was young," he says. "I spent a year of my life studying with Louis Kahn. He set up ethical principals about how to treat materials. You insult the material if you don't use it properly."

Even so, Cutler considers homes to be little more than backdrops for human life. He returned to the site for a wedding a year after it was built. "It was a rainy day, with the typical Northwest gray mist of a rain. There were about 150 people in the house. The big vertical lift doors were all open. The couple was at the opposite end of the pond, with umbrellas held over their head. The sound of the ceremony was carrying over the pond and collecting in the pitch of the roof. I turned to my wife and said, 'This is exactly why I do this—to create stage sets for people to live their life.'"

A covered entry leads to a front door with a focused view of the Rocky Mountains. *Photo by John J. Macaulay/Johnsen Schmaling Architects*

The inclined roof on Johnsen Schmaling's Mountain House references distant ski slopes. *Photo by John J. Macaulay/ Johnsen Schmaling Architects*

Open stairs in the entry provide a glimpse of the second floor. The stairs terminate in a small observatory. *Photo by John J. Macaulay/Johnsen Schmaling Architects*

IT'S SUBLIME WHEN HUMAN SHELTER INTERTWINES WITH LIFE'S MEMORABLE MOMENTS. But even a home built to the most stringent environmental standards leaves a scar on the earth. Forests are cut to provide lumber, granite quarried to create countertops, gypsum mined to manufacture drywall. Energy is consumed to make and transport the materials. Then they are collected to form a building on what may have formerly been a pristine spot of ground, disrupting the views all around, interrupting the natural order. In the worst case, an entire neighborhood of insensitively designed homes takes over what used to be forested ground.

A desire to protect views of the natural landscape drives Schmaling. He sympathizes with locals who, driving through the countryside on a weekend afternoon, may get riled to see a new home where a farm or woods used to be. Even a home designed to the highest environmental standard, made entirely of sustainable materials, designed to produce all the energy it needs to consume, could still be considered a blight on the earth's surface.

"We need to consider the visual impact of what we build, especially when we touch land that hasn't been touched for a long time," says Schmaling. "You need to be respectful to the people who have to look at it. You can't do it the cheap way so that it becomes an aesthetic pollutant. Homes should become part of the land rather than sit on it. You have a responsibility to the people who will live in the building as well. They need to be able enjoy the landscape. They want to breathe it, like the air."

Schmaling's Mountain House in Montana succeeds on both scores. A lengthy sustainability agenda started with the decision to build on the foundation of an obsolete building, damaged beyond repair by neglect and decades of exposure to rough mountain climate conditions. Set within the crest of a hill, the home appears embedded in the foothills of Wilson Peak, even as it serves up views of the Rocky Mountains. A low, sloping profile follows the land with a series of flat and gently pitched volumes and planes. The roof mimics a ski jump and echoes gondola rides in the distance.

Once again, Schmaling carefully choreographed the entry sequence, since it's the best chance to make a strong first impression. Visitors descend from an outdoor parking area into a sunken courtyard protected from snow and rain by a wood canopy. The confined space leads to a large pivot door that opens to an entry vestibule with a framed mountain view. The entry links the major rooms on the first floor—kitchen, dining room, and bedrooms. Custom sliding doors, picture windows, and pivot doors ensure unobstructed mountain views in each room.

Overhangs, trellises, and decks turn the home's outdoor spaces into a veritable amphitheater. *Photo by John J. Macaulay/Johnsen Schmaling Architects*

First-floor rooms open to a long south-facing terrace with a deep, protective overhang and trellises. An intertwined system of outdoor spaces—covered patios, louvered terraces, and courtyards—creates a buffer between indoor and outdoor spaces. It's as though the architect created an amphitheater for viewing the alpine scenery.

An exterior palette of muted browns, grays, and silver makes the house virtually disappear into the mountain landscape. Unfinished cedar cladding, charred to bring out a natural preservative that protects against rot, insects, and climate extremes, blends with the color and texture of surrounding trees. The process, called shou sugi ban, extends the life of the siding up to eighty years and produces a silver-black surface—a pleasant contrast to clear cedar and corrugated steel cladding that will one day turn ferrous. The highly textured home will age gracefully.

THE OPTIMAL ORIENTATION OF A HOUSE ISN'T ALWAYS AS OBVIOUS AS IT WAS WITH THE MOUNTAIN HOUSE.
The challenge for Richard Williams, in the case of a home and guest house he designed for a retired couple in rural Virginia, called Fletcher's Mill, was how to maximize multiple views—a meadow, woods, river, and three nearby Blue Ridge Mountain peaks. The architect repeatedly visited the site—a knoll tucked into the edge of the woods, overlooking a meadow gently

Architect Richard Williams studied hard to pick the ideal site for Fletcher's Mill, a minimalist interpretation of a Virginia farmhouse composed with a limited palette of concrete, cedar, and bluestone. *Photo by Tom Arban*

sloping down to the Thornton River—to visualize how he might orient rooms, windows, and porches. He was aided by three-dimensional computer simulation that showed windowed views from inside computer-generated rooms.

The couple wanted a home so desirable that it would draw frequent visits by children and grandchildren. But the home couldn't be too big—it had to work for the empty nesters on a daily basis, too. Further complicating the design mission, the couple raises cattle and grows vegetables on the property. So the home had to function as a farmhouse, with space provided for dirty boots, business management, equipment storage, and animal husbandry. Williams ultimately designed a compound—a 4,900-square-foot main house, with an 850-square-foot guesthouse, a 620-square-foot tool shed/studio, and a pool.

Williams decided the best spot for the house would be on a knoll bordered by the woods, a vantage that would provide the best views up the mountainside and down to the meadow. He turned the house slightly, so that it heels into the slope of the meadow. The orientation allowed him to connect two living levels to the ground, a technique used in the region's historic bank barns. The arrangement not only makes it more convenient to enter the home with dirty boots but cools the house as well.

Williams' thinking about the floor plan began in an unconventional place—the screened porch. "The design of a screen porch is often an afterthought," says Williams. "But it's the place where you'd want to be at all times of the day during all but the harshest weather. It was our starting point for the organization of the house. It occupies the choicest point on the

Rolling barn doors, highly appropriate in a farmhouse, separate an office from the great room. *Photo by Tom Arban*

A hallway, complete with a bench to tie shoes and store work boots, frames views of mountain peaks at both ends. *Photo by Tom Arban*

Williams plotted a prime location for the back porch, knowing its importance to country retreats. *Photo by Tom Arban*

A brick fireplace and sturdy tile floors seem right at home in the updated farmhouse. *Photo by Tom Arban*

entire property, embracing tall meadow grasses and small trees, and it provides a mountain view." The principal of Richard Williams Architects also made sure the porch could be easily accessed from the main living spaces and the kitchen.

Principle living spaces, each with a river view, line a long hallway that frames views of mountain peaks at either end. Subtle changes in wall, floor, and ceiling finishes provide transitions from one room to the next. The great room looks down to a river meadow to the south and up to the mountain path and upper meadow to the north. Walls of square insulated windows draw borders around views. A long bench, the ideal spot for taking off and storing work boots, sits under a window wall by the back door. Polished concrete and stone flooring make it easy to sweep up.

The house consists of three basic forms anchored by a tall painted brick chimney. Niches carved out of thick exterior walls store logs, tools, and agricultural supplies. Materials carried from outside to inside blur the boundaries between indoor and outdoor space, making the home feel more at home on the mountainside. In the great room, large floor tile and a built-in bookcase reference a square window pattern. It's easy to miss that a door leading to the meadow is carved out of the window wall. A simple painted brick fireplace creates the ambiance of a mountain home.

ON THE OPPOSITE SIDE OF THE COUNTRY, architect Jeffrey Berkus, whose firm bears his name, concentrates on how the sun and moon, and patterns of light and shadow, influence a sense of place. His homes reflect their surroundings in a literal sense. He often draws large south-facing clerestory windows that serve as timekeepers, casting light on walls and interior spaces. Direct sunlight may reach deep into the house in winter. But a reflection may be all you get in the summer. And all this varies by time of day, too. "People who live in my homes tell me they are more aware of the seasons," he says.

The 201 House by Jeffrey Berkus Architects playfully riffs on the gabled forms and bay windows of Aspen's downtown Victorian neighborhoods. *Photo by Studiocota*

Berkus brought that objective to an Aspen home for a husband-and-wife team who film architectural documentaries around the world. The daylighting challenge at the 201 House was heightened by the client's desire for a basement with a lounge and two bedrooms for their children. The request was a response to an Aspen design ordinance that restricts a home's footprint based on its lot size, a regulatory approach showing up more frequently in high-growth areas. In this case, the ordinance restricted the owners to 3,600 square feet of floor space on their 9,000-square-foot lot. Because the number doesn't include basements, homeowners often resort to building out that level as living space.

The problem, as Berkus well knew, is that lower levels won't get used often unless they receive lots of natural light. He took care of that by designing a large south-facing window wall (seven feet by twenty feet) at the top of an open stairwell; it throws light deep into the lower level. Though twelve feet under ground, the basement feels completely connected to the sun and lines of view on the main floor. "I went there for a Super Bowl party," says Berkus. "Everyone outside could see the game down below. And from down below, you could see the people outside. It worked well."

The window wall, which strategically frames views of ski slopes, casts shadows on a living room wall that change by time of day and year. As he likes to do, Berkus employed the geometry of the golden section, 1×1.618, in the design of the living room. This seemingly universal pattern underlies the design of everything from nautiluses, to honey combs, to ancient churches. "It influences all our work," he says. "It's the proportion of blood vessels branching out from the heart, and branches from trees. It's why people feel so connected. It's phenomenal how it activates people."

The home's exterior echoes the gables, bay windows, and front porches that form downtown Aspen's Victorian vernacular. But that's about as far as the comparison goes. Unusual geometry and sleek, almost industrial, materials combine to create a contemporary impression. Harsh mountain weather called for super-durable siding. Berkus used a treated wood, ipe, in alternate courses of two and four inches. The architect has visited the home several times since it was completed to see how the siding is holding up. "It's bullet-proof, and it bounces light instead of absorbing it," he says.

If the couple wanted a house that blended with its surroundings, they also wanted it to work for parties. Berkus made sure that the main living areas—the living and dining rooms, and the kitchen—each had two entrances so partyers never get stuck in a crowded room. To further facilitate circulation, public rooms directly connect to outdoor patios and decks. Visitors may not venture outside, even if a room is crowded, if the porch can only be reached through a bedroom or dining nook. The home accommodates a variety of furniture arrangements—intimate spaces for friends to reacquaint and open spaces to mingle and make new friends. The location of sofas and hors d'oeuvre settings may not matter to people who don't entertain often. But if that's the lifestyle you lead, details such as furniture arrangements and circulation patterns can make a huge difference.

4.
ANTICIPATE
EVOLVING
LIFESTYLES

FAMILY CIRCUMSTANCES CHANGE; THE BEST HOMES CAN ADAPT

A great home built today would have many things in common with one built 100 or 150 years ago. It might be constructed with the same raw materials—limestone, brick, and wood—used to build homes for centuries. It would need to respond to the same forces of wind, sun, and water, and it may even do so in a similar fashion. But that wouldn't be enough. Today's home designs must take advantage of modern products, systems, and engineering. Plus, they need to accommodate, if not anticipate, evolving lifestyles. Designers in the 1920s and 1930s didn't have to consider how people would use computers, tablets, and smartphones at home, own three cars, recycle cans and bottles, entertain friends in the kitchen of all places, or watch live soccer matches from the other side of the world on a television the size of a picture window.

The biggest change from the old days may be that households spend most of their time living on the backside of the home. At the turn of the twentieth century, the most occupied rooms were relegated to the front, close to the street, where visitors left their horse or car. Sitting in the front parlor or living room, families could keep one eye on the street, see the comings and goings of the neighborhood. Visitors were ushered into the foyer where they would be treated with glimpses of an elegant furnished living room to one side, a resplendent dining room to the other, and a grand staircase in the middle. These traditional elements said you had arrived, both literally and figuratively.

"Life styles have changed a lot in the last one hundred years," says Stephen Muse, principle of Muse Architects, who is sometimes called in to redesign homes from bygone eras. "The garage was often detached and buried in the backyard where no one would see it. These days everyone wants a family room and a kitchen in the back and a garage in the front. The house has been flipped."

To be sure, great room plans with combined living spaces and kitchens along the back are the norm in new homes. People prefer an informal living space—especially one that connects to a porch, deck, or patio—that they can shape to suit their needs. Kitchens, with the addition of islands, have become the hub of family activity. Only the largest, most luxurious homes contain formal dining and living rooms these days.

THIS DESIRE FOR A MODERN LIFESTYLE GUIDED MUSE'S RECENT DESIGN of a home on a tight suburban Maryland lot for an empty-nester couple—an artist and an economist. The couple intend to one day move here from Chicago to be closer to their daughter and grandchildren. The house and lot were certainly big enough to have included formal dining and living rooms. But the couple decided on an open plan instead. A kitchen wall divides informal from more formal space. On one side, a television wall anchors the kitchen and family room. The other holds slightly more formal space for conversation and dining.

The two-story glass front of this house makes a dramatic, though somewhat misleading first impression. It mostly reveals a second-floor hallway in what's actually a very private home. Most public spaces in the U-shaped design look out to a rear courtyard, with a private terrace, garden, lawn, and pool to one side. Garden walls envelope the courtyard. Few windows face neighboring homes to either side. But the house is flooded with light thanks to the window well in front and copious patio doors and windows facing the courtyard.

The view from the entry is carefully arranged. Visitors step inside what feels like a glass box with a bench to remove their shoes and a painting by the "artist in residence." "One step to the right, into the living room, and you see the backyard," says Muse. "If there is a great view to the back, ninety-nine percent of architects put a lot of glass back there. The question is how you set that up. . . . It's a great feeling to step into a wonderful house. It's like the feeling that you get when you are watching a movie and halfway through you realize, this is a great movie."

Varied roofing treatments—a metal roof on the two-story main building and less formal wood shingles on the one-story wings—break down the mass of what would otherwise be perceived as a very large home. The technique makes the wings resemble garden sheds or later additions attached later. A pavilion that houses an artist studio features a hipped roof common to Chicago homes. A ground-floor master bedroom and an office round out the first floor. Stairs at one end of the house lead to a gallery hallway on the second floor lined with bedrooms.

Glass, monolithic white interiors, and the home's external orientation combine to create a modern impression. But the home—clad with local fieldstone, stained siding, and wall shingles—may be more accurately classified as updated Prairie style. Stainless steel gutters appear at regular intervals to break down the building's mass. Symmetrically arranged windows are ganged into groups of one, two, or three. In the Prairie style, most windows on the building wings feature smaller high and low panes that sandwich a big middle panel with unobstructed views.

All the glass could lead to overheating in the summer were it not for the deep overhangs, trellises, and pocketed roller shades. Exposing most rooms to at least two exterior walls provides cross ventilation, minimizing the need for air conditioning. The highly energy efficient home includes a heating, ventilation, and air conditioning system that recycles energy; a strategic combination of more expensive open-cell and less expensive closed-cell foam insulation; and windows and doors that retain heat on cold winter days.

A media wall separates formal from informal spaces. Sliding glass doors open to a regimented interior courtyard with spaces for conversation, contemplation, and dining. © *Maxwell MacKenzie*

An open stairwell, placed at one end of the house where it won't interfere with views, leads to bedrooms upstairs. © *Maxwell MacKenzie*

The previous home on this lot sat right in the middle, exposed on four sides. Muse pushed the wings of the new home to the lot line on either side, creating more room for a private courtyard in the middle. He made the lawn the center of attention in the courtyard rather than a pool that's covered most months of the year. Sidewalks with grass growing between pavers soften the transition from the house to the courtyard. Evenings might begin at the far patio adjacent to a fire pit and a pool. Then dinner might be served at a more private second patio close to the kitchen and enclosed by the home's wings.

THE BEST HOMES TODAY MAKE THE MOST OF OUTDOOR SPACES, a movement presaged by modernist architects working after WWII. The most famous homes from this era—the Case Study houses designed in the hills of Los Angeles by the country's leading architects—featured large glass expanses that provided awe-inspiring views of hills and canyons. These days the walls between house and nature are literally coming down, or rolling back. Architects and builders have found affordable ways to link great rooms and patios with sliding or folding glass doors, a trend that infiltrated production homes in the early 2000s. Now upscale production homes may include entire outdoor rooms— complete with grills, refrigerators, conversation pits, and dining tables—that connect seamlessly with interior spaces.

As family life evolves, so do home designs. Witness the Buena Vista House that California architect Kevin deFreitas designed for his sister's family of five in Redwood City, a few miles north of Paolo Alto. They wanted to update a 1,440-square-foot midcentury modern home developed by Joseph Eichler. The family's extremely active lifestyle includes 100-mile bike races and hiking and camping in the national forests. High on the wish list was a giant garage to hold camping gear and a collection of eight bikes, some for commuting. The wish list also included an open kitchen and family room. The family entertains frequently and his sister loves to cook. "But that was really it in terms of what they wanted," says deFreitas, whose firm bears his name.

The design, like the Eichler home before it, focuses interior views on a rear courtyard, conveniently shielded on three sides by mature trees. The main public rooms are arranged in an L-shape, as in the existing plan, and look out to the courtyard. Subtle changes—a lower ceiling over the kitchen, different ceiling material in the family room—mark transitions between rooms. Other touches—wood details repeated in the kitchen and a built-in family room buffet, for instance—tie the spaces together.

With a mere eight feet separating homes in the neighborhood, privacy is a big concern. Kitchen windows in the previous home looked directly into the neighbor's house. DeFreitas used a fireplace wall to block the view of one neighboring house. He carefully located windows on the opposite side to create privacy but also permit natural light to enter. In fact, solar radiation through the home's many windows provides one hundred percent of the home's daylight needs until sundown.

Some Eichler homes emphasize privacy at the expense of being a good neighbor. DeFreitas wanted this home to make a friendlier impression. He clad it with warm redwood siding and pre-painted metal, and specified a translucent, glow-in-the-dark garage door. He also included more windows than the typical Eichler to link the home to the street. The two-inch redwood siding on the remodeled house was salvaged from an old water tank. The architect loves its patina. "It is absolutely stunning in person, super rich in color with all the mineral streaking and remnants from its water storage days," he says.

The vegetarian family entertains often—they may have three or four families over—and deFreitas's sister, who has transitioned out of the high-tech world into being a stay-at-home mom, loves to cook and bake. He created kitchen prep space for the boys to help their mom prepare a meal. "The boys want to be where she is," says deFreitas, adding that his sister also wants to keep tabs on her boys' screen time. From the kitchen island she can monitor computer use in a homework space, separated from the family room only by a pocket door.

White walls provide a canvas for art and choice architectural details. A concrete fireplace wall is done with the same concrete technique used to form the exterior walls. Corner windows, little more than butted glass recessed into the wall, create great sitting spots. Floor-to-ceiling glass in the dining room looks out to a Zen garden, a detail borrowed from homes done in the mid-twentieth century. An invisible window frame—it's buried in gravel outside the wall—makes it difficult to tell whether the garden is inside or out. The family decided to spend their money on this architectural details instead of art.

DeFreitas prefers a clean interiors approach to a craftsman style home, which is often so rich in detail that "your eye goes everywhere." The good thing about white walls is that they accommodate virtually any kind of furnishing. Instead of a traditional armoire, which deFreitas thinks would have worked, the family bought modern furniture, including a Saarinen womb chair, a Barcelona chair, and translucent rubber light fixtures designed by George Nelson, one of Eames's professors. They glow like Japanese lanterns.

DeFreitas feels a special obligation to every client, even those who aren't family members. It's a very personal experience to design a home. "The family home becomes the backdrop for many life-long memories: birthday parties, adventurous departures, celebratory returns, broken windows, stitches . . . or just a place to lie on the couch staring at the ceiling and dreaming," he says. "So it should be a good ceiling."

Families may also entrust an architect with their fortune, since so much personal equity is tied up in the house. That's no small burden. Families deserve a home that's flexible enough to change with their lifestyle—when children come and go, when income rises and falls, or when mobility, eyesight, or hearing start to deteriorate. The latter is especially

important because, to accommodate a disability, families may incur a big remodeling expense when they can least afford it, when they are older or medical bills are pouring in.

Families also deserve a safe home that will prevent the kinds of accidents—broken hips and legs—that render some homes unusable. One thing to consider is that many home accidents occur on stairs. Some result from magazines, clothes baskets, or bathroom supplies left on a bottom or top stair. Why not provide storage spots on landings? Bathroom falls are another big cause of injury. It makes sense to specify slip-resistant tile, along with a grab bar in the shower to catch your fall and scald-resistant showerheads to prevent accidental burns. If you do fall, your head is better able to take a blow from a rounded corner than the angular bathroom hardware that caught your fancy.

The statistics are sobering: a full 21.3 percent of the US population has some kind of disability, whether it's bad hearing, sight, or immobility. The figure rises to more than fifty percent of Americans sixty-five and older, according to the US Census. Disability can occur suddenly or gradually; it pays to be prepared in either case. A first-floor bedroom, or at least the ability to inexpensively carve one out of existing space, may become a godsend if climbing the stairs becomes an ordeal. Since you may one day need to change a kitchen sink to fit a wheelchair beneath it, why not run floor tile all the way to the wall under base cabinets when you first build a home? That way you won't have to bring in a tile setter later.

New homes built for the disabled address mundane tasks that the able-bodied take for granted. They consider how the disabled person needs to dress for work, bathe a child, take a shower, or clean up after a party. Even healthy family

The family room leads to a private terraced back porch with zoned conversation pits for children to escape parents, and vice versa.
Photo by Darren Bradley

PLANS / *Courtesy deFreitas Architects*

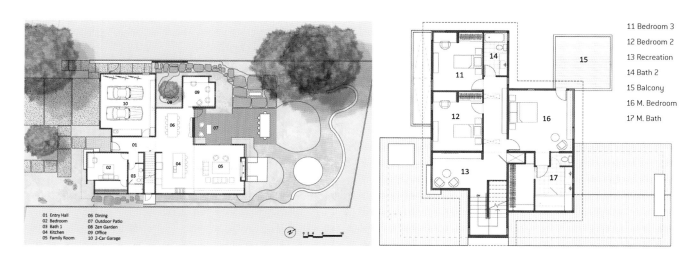

01 Entry Hall
02 Bedroom
03 Bath 1
04 Kitchen
05 Family Room
06 Dining
07 Outdoor Patio
08 Zen Garden
09 Office
10 2-Car Garage

11 Bedroom 3
12 Bedroom 2
13 Recreation
14 Bath 2
15 Balcony
16 M. Bedroom
17 M. Bath

members would be well advised to think about the preferred method for performing common tasks. There's no reason why a home shouldn't be as ergonomically comfortable as a new luxury automobile, with everything within easy reach. How do you prefer to store your clothes? In open shelves, on hangers, in a dresser? Where do you prefer to tie your shoes? In your bedroom? By the door?

Nearly everyone's vision eventually degrades, sometimes to the point where you wished you had designed your home differently. Aging baby boomers are already pushing back against white kitchens with stainless steel appliances. In open plans with tons of natural light, shiny surfaces may produce a glare that makes it tough to see. Appliances with a matte finish, indirect lighting, and window coverings may be a better option. Architects love to tie together rooms in open floor plans with a single style of flooring. But contrasting color and texture on floors, walls, and ceilings makes them easier to see. That's particularly important at changes in floor grade.

Noise can become a nuisance in an open home with too many hard surfaces. One in seventeen Americans suffer from hearing loss. They are sensitive to ambient noise that makes it difficult to hear others talking. Hard parallel surfaces—a tile floor and wall, for instance—create an echo effect that makes rooms noisier. Naturally it makes sense to separate noisy home theaters and great rooms from bedrooms and offices. Carpeting, drapes, wall hangings, and acoustic ceiling tile also reduce noise transfer. The benefits to acoustic design go beyond better hearing. Studies show that controlling noise reduces stress. And a big reason people love their home is because it provides a sanctuary from tension.

Too often, people building a new home fall in love with the latest trend and make decisions they may regret later: floor tiles that are hard on the knees, recessed lights that are difficult to change, or fancy doorknobs that are difficult to turn. Universal design can help guide decision-making. This voluntary standard produces a home that people of all ages and abilities should be able to use comfortably, even those using a walker or wheelchair. Many of these design touches, like raising electrical outlets so they are easier to reach, are invisible to the unpracticed eye. Some make eminent sense regardless of your abilities, like raising the dishwasher so that it's easier to load or putting a pullout shelf under a wall oven. That way you can easily and immediately put down a hot pan or dish.

UNIVERSAL DESIGN DROVE THE REMAKE OF A 1960S-STYLE RANCH HOUSE IN PALO ALTO that Paula Krugmeier, a principal of BAR Architects, did for an empty-nester couple who wanted a smaller, more usable home than the McMansions in the neighborhood. The Greenwoods had lived through an experience with a parent forced to leave the house she loved because she couldn't manage the stairs. The couple had even cared for a wheelchair-bound relative in their previous house. They understood the universal design details that would make the biggest difference. They didn't want visible hallmarks such as institutional-looking grab bars, exposed plumbing under the sink, or wheelchair lifts. But they wanted to be prepared for the day when they may need those things.

Krugmeier started by creating a flush front entry with a generous eave that completely protects exterior paving from the elements. The path slopes gently from the house, directing rain away. She charted a generous, well-lit path through the house, eliminating interior door thresholds, and designed wide hallways and door jambs. (Many homeowners must

A lush courtyard cools key rooms.
Photo by Doug Dun/BAR Architects.

The home centers around a large
kitchen island with low counters,
three sinks, and built-in seating.
Photo by Doug Dun/BAR Architect

A threshold-free shower, roll-up space
under the sink, and ample clearance
around the toilet ensure that the
master bath will always be usable.
Photo by Doug Dun/BAR Architects

PLANS / Staggered boxy forms
produce five courtyards, each with
a different intended use. *Photo by
Doug Dun/BAR Architects*

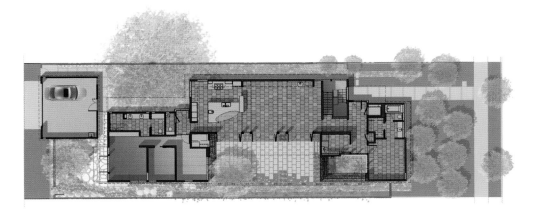

eventually widen doorways to thirty-six inches to navigate them with a walker, scooter, or wheelchair.) Many doors slide back into pockets or stack along a wall, making them easier to operate from a sitting position than a swinging door. They also don't use as much floor space.

The architect raised electrical outlets and lowered light switches so that everyone, including children and adults who have trouble bending over, can reach them. She lowered counter heights (thirty-four inches instead of the usual thirty-six) to make them easier to reach, raised the dishwasher, and specified levered handle sets that can be operated with the push of a hand or elbow. A swiveling breakfast bar, dubbed the surfboard due to its long, elliptical shape, could be easily reached from a wheelchair. The master bath has enough open space to navigate in a walker. The couple went for a test drive before moving in, successfully driving a rented wheelchair around the house.

The drive took them on a pleasant journey through strategically sited courtyards. Three bifold doors, left open for most of the year, merge the living/dining/kitchen space with the main outdoor courtyard, heavily planted to passively cool the house during the summer. A private, first-level master suite enjoys its own south-facing courtyard. It's an ideal spot to retreat to when the Greenwood's children and their families come to visit.

The floor plan includes two guest suites—one on the main level, another in the basement. A south-facing light well channels light into the basement, which includes a kitchenette and living area in addition to a bedroom and en suite bath. A glazed wall acoustically separates the suite and also provides a secondary source of illumination through the stairs. The basement suite turned out to be extremely useful for the Greenwoods. At various times it has accommodated each of their daughters with their families for up to a year without turmoil.

Since the Greenwoods both work from home, they wanted a home that would be comfortable both day and night without the use of mechanical air conditioning. Krugmeier included a host of passive cooling and heating strategies to regulate indoor air temperatures. Strategically located windows and light shelves bounce light into interior spaces, reducing the need for artificial illumination. Sunshades block direct sun from the East. Overhangs and light shelves shade westerly clerestories.

A steeply pitched roof descends to cover an integrated, shaded front porch on this private Nashville residence by Carson Looney. *Photo by Nick McGinn*

Floor-level awning windows in the courtyard can be opened at night to admit air cooled by evaporation in the garden area. The cool air lowers the temperature of the interior concrete slab and stone tile. The windows can be closed in the morning to maintain the coolness of the slab and regulate internal temperatures. Meanwhile, a white roof, nearly invisible from the street, reflects heat back into the sky. A walnut tree shades a south-facing breakfast area in the summer. When its leaves fall in the winter, sunlight heats the spot. Cross drafts—produced by opening low awning windows on one side and high windows on the opposite side—cool the home in shoulder seasons. In-floor heating keeps the house at even temperatures in the winter. Rooftop photovoltaic panels supply electricity; solar collectors generate hot water.

MANY PEOPLE BALANCE UNIVERSAL DESIGN AGAINST AESTHETIC CONSIDERATIONS to arrive at their dream home. Case in point is a Nashville infill home architect Carson Looney designed for an empty-nester couple moving down from a much larger suburban home. The couple, though active and healthy, was well aware that their condition could change. When presented with a list universal design techniques, they selected only the ones that would improve the livability of their home now.

Most living space in the 3,100-square-foot house is conveniently located on the ground level, including the master suite. There's easy flow and circulation between the first-floor spaces designed for entertaining and extended family. Looney, as a matter of course, widens doorways to thirty-six inches and designs hallways at least four feet wide. Galleries in the front and rear, at four foot, six inches, are roomy enough to pass through with luggage or packages without hitting the walls.

The threshold to the shower in the master bath is curbless, and there's enough room for a seat, should it be necessary to add one later. Floor tile under the sink in the bathroom and kitchen runs all the way to the wall, so that if you'd ever want a roll-up sink it wouldn't require a major remodel. Solid blocking behind bathroom walls in key spots—in the shower, around the toilet—allows support hardware to be installed later. Benches in the master closet are ideal for sitting down to tie shoes. Light switches were lowered to elbow height, and outlets at cabinets and vanities were positioned at the most comfortable height for the owners.

The steep drop of the site from front to back created a potential accessibility problem. Looney decided to fill a portion of the drive and garage to raise it within a foot of the main floor level. He then added some easy steps with four-inch risers and sixteen-inch treads with enough length that they could be covered by a ramp, if need be. He also made sure to leave enough room in the garage for two cars to fit comfortably when their doors are open. That way you don't have to turn sideways to exit the car or contort your body to extricate groceries or luggage.

The big idea in this house may be the do-all utility room on the first floor. Naturally lit by a generous bank of windows, the space is home to daily and seasonal activities that are often overlooked. It's a spot for the washer and dryer, an office desk, file storage, a sewing table, bulk storage, and pet feeding. A center island

A vaulted ceiling adds drama and texture to the living room. *Photo by Nick McGinn*

Patio doors open to a screened porch, complete with a fireplace for cool evenings and a ceiling fan for hot summer days. *Photo by Nick McGinn*

A brightly lit "do-all" utility room allocates space for nearly any household chore. *Photo by Nick McGinn*

is set at the perfect height to fold laundry, wrap gifts, and do craft projects. Rather than relegate it to dead space in the floor plan, Looney designed the do-all room into the home's circulation pattern, connecting it to the garage and the master bedroom. To get there you don't have to pass through the main living spaces. That way, guests won't see you taking dirty laundry or holiday presents into the do-all room.

The home's mostly white interiors made glare a potential concern. Looney designed roofs over the porch in front and the outdoor room in back to provide deep shading, and he balanced the natural light entering key rooms by providing multiple windows. "The biggest source of glare is when you have windows on only one wall of a room," he says. Balancing light to fight glare may not seem like a big deal now. But it could easily become one later, when the problem is much more expensive to fix.

5.
FRESHLY INTERPRET
TRADITION

Nostalgic neighborhoods in England and Los Gatos, California, inspired the traditional home designs at Laurel Mews. *Photo courtesy of Robson Homes*

Rapt attention to authentic detailing—bay windows, planter boxes, and porch columns—made the bungalows a favorite of high-tech executives. *Photo courtesy of Robson Homes*

THE BEST HOMES TAKE FAMILIAR FORMS AND MATERIALS TO A NEW LEVEL

As a teenager, architect David Ko used to ride the bus to Westwood, Glendale, and other Los Angeles neighborhoods built in the 1920s and 1930s, the Golden Age of American architecture. He'd ask the driver to stop mid-block so that he could take pictures of classic Tudor, Spanish colonial, and Italian revival-style homes that caught his fancy. By dissecting old architectural plan books in the public library, he developed a gift for visualizing the interiors of homes, often by focusing on key exterior details—the location of the back door, turrets, or bay windows. Architects who drew the grandest homes in the country used to publish their drawings for the greater good of American architecture. Ko, who now buys old plan books instead of checking them out of the library, still finds inspiration in their classic details and proportions. Like many architects, he also travels the world for inspiration.

The nostalgic neighborhoods of Los Gatos, California, and cobblestone lanes in Great Britain provided the design cues for one of Ko's award-winning projects, Laurel Mews, a subdivision of twenty-two traditional homes in the Silicon Valley on the two-acre site of a former used car lot. One home in the community, a 3,100-square-foot California arts and crafts shingle style house, won home of the year in a thirteen-state western home competition. Rarely are production homes designed with so many authentic details—everything from bracketed eaves to bay windows with roof overhangs. High-tech executives quickly bought the homes, which they decided were extraordinary but wouldn't call attention to their wealth.

Architects lament the difficulty of designing traditional homes correctly, especially when working with penny-pinching clients. Budgets may not provide the leeway to properly replicate cornice trim, porch columns, and gable ends. But Laurel Mews could be an exception because of the wealth of potential buyers. It's characterized by authentic rooflines that slope down to generous front porches supported with appropriate columns. Picket fences enclose courtyards, creating the appeal of a cottage neighborhood.

Ko held back on interior details, though they are still done in a craftsman style. Unpretentious baseboard molding winds its way up walls to wrap windows and doors, defining hanging storage areas for coats and backpacks along the way, just

as you would see in traditional arts and crafts homes built on site by hand. A boxed beam and beaded wood ceiling differentiates the living room from others in the open plan. Wide-panel oak flooring unites the spaces, creating a traditional white-and-brown color scheme. Sunken-panel cabinets in the kitchen echo the panels in a Dutch back door.

Built-in sitting areas were often the most prized aspect of bungalow designs. Ko, principal of Angeleno Associates, bumped out exterior walls to create an intimate sitting room with windows on three sides. It's an ideal place to watch your children play outside or see what's going on in the neighborhood. The master suite includes a built-in reading nook that would be an ideal place to nurse a child. The windowed second-floor laundry room includes a craft corner, with hangers to hold rolls of wrapping paper. A fully built-out basement includes a bar, bath, and media room.

Ko's pet peeve is that modern homes ignore usable square footage under the roof. What makes many older homes special is that architects employed every cubic inch, especially on the top floor, where they designed low-ceilinged spaces that fit snugly under the roof, an opportunity that's often lost when trusses are just dropped over the second floor. At Laurel Mews, clipped roofs resulted in bedroom ceilings that slope to the wall, creating sitting areas that are ideal for reading or napping.

THESE DAYS BUILDERS AND ARCHITECTS LOOKING TO DESIGN GREAT TRADITIONAL HOMES are more likely to take guidance from community pattern books. Often commissioned by design-conscious developers, the books illustrate everything from acceptable quoin details to how chimneys should meet the ground. Most require shutters to be sized to match the width and height of windows, so that they can at least appear to close. The size and pitch of roof dormers needs to relate to the home's gables. Window styles and openings should be appropriate to the architecture of the home.

Problems arise when homebuyers want an overly impressive front side. They may ask for large columns out of proportion with the height of the home. Another temptation is to use as many siding materials as possible, now that faux stone can be stuck on for decoration. Some architects take advice from the world's most elegant woman, Coco Chanel, who was said to have advised when dressing with accessories, "Before you leave the house, look in the mirror and take one thing off." Homes sometimes try to do too much on the front, then fail to articulate the rear or side that people see less often. The result: a home that looks like a stage prop.

One of the most inspired examples of fresh traditional architecture can be found in Alys Beach along the Gulf Coast of Florida, next door to Seaside and Rosemary Beach, two other celebrated communities. While these older traditional neighborhood developments (TNDs) are striking, nothing prepares you for Alys Beach. Derived from the architecture of

Bermuda and of Antigua Guatemala, the colonial capital of Central America, the community's architectural guidelines call for uniform white walls and roofs. If the uniformity is picturesque, it's also practical, reflecting the sun's heat to cool the seaside town. Only 899 homes will be built there, more than half of them detached.

Lintels, piers, buttresses, and beams articulate walls. They combine to form either windows and doors or larger elements such as porches, loggias, and courtyards, and support projected elements like balconies and chimneys. The structural elements are countered by lighter materials—aged wood railings and shutters, metal-framed awnings, and draped curtains that shade and protect the homes. It's one thing to design a single house in this fashion. When it's done on every home it creates singular beauty.

The design code restricts the width of Gulf-front homes so that more households can enjoy ocean views. It also requires that they include a center or side courtyard, with no side, rear, or front yards. As a consolation, homes in this corridor may rise to three stories. Bigger ones often include rooftop porches or decks to enjoy ocean views and Gulf breezes. And nearly all the homes carefully integrate indoor and outdoor spaces in old-school ways to promote natural ventilation. Cool air enters through first-story windows and loggias, circulating to upper floors through courtyards and stairwells with the help of ceiling fans.

FIRST FLOOR PLAN
HOUSE RESIDENCE

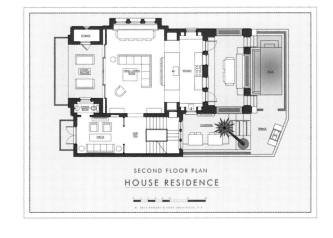

SECOND FLOOR PLAN
HOUSE RESIDENCE

THIRD FLOOR PLAN
HOUSE RESIDENCE

The House house, designed by town architects Marieanne Khoury and Erik Vogt for an Atlanta family of four, sits within the waterfront zone, four blocks from the ocean. The logical place for the living and dining rooms would have been an upper floor where the views would be better. But elevating public rooms would have made it difficult to connect them to an outdoor courtyard. The partners decided to raise the courtyard, too. In so doing, they created a path for cool ocean breezes to wind their way through interior rooms. "Six months of the year the temperature is wonderful," says Khoury. "But when it's very hot, you want air to continually move through the house."

The configuration creates an unusual circulatory pattern for humans. From the entry, a half flight of stairs takes you to a lower courtyard with an alfresco fireplace—a nice place to chill after a day at the beach. Steps rise from here to a second court with a summer kitchen; it's located next to a raised dipping pool where the family could spend an entire afternoon if they grow tired of the beach. Another short flight of stairs leads from the pool to a dining loggia adjacent to the second-floor kitchen. This is the scenic way to reach the public areas of the house—you could also take a second flight of stairs directly to the second-floor living areas.

The interior opens to the wind like a boat, with draperies for sails. French doors or lift-and-slide doors open most second-story spaces to sea breezes. Windows on the leeward side provide cross-ventilation. Another family room—this one on the third floor—opens on three sides to provide sweeping views of the Gulf and the town. After working at Alys Beach for more than a decade, "the idea of not creating outdoor rooms is anathema to me," Khoury says. All told, the 3,667-square-foot home includes 582 square feet in covered loggias and porches. "We could have built out to 4,500 square feet, but that would have affected how the family lives in the house," she says.

The home is ready for the beach. An independent first-floor master suite provides guest quarters for visiting family or friends. Storage for beach equipment rounds out the first floor. The home contains a traditional child's bedroom and a second bedroom with four bunk beds served by a ship ladder. The interiors embrace an eclectic seaside aesthetic, with touches of glamour. A draped entry pulls back to reveal ball lights dripping from the staircase ceiling. Upstairs, draped awnings separate the loggia from indoor spaces. "We just love drapes," says Khoury. "They create privacy even as air circulates around them. They add so much to a room. They complete the look, almost like jewelry on a woman. Plus, they play with light and shadow, and they move with the wind, which is very evocative when you are close to the water."

The interiors keep the promise made by the exteriors. Moorish style wood screens in the family room echo façade details. Old-world Venetian plaster reflects light differently at various times of day, shimmering subtly at night. An overscaled black light fixture in the living room contrasts with light marble countertops. Linen and cotton upholstery provides a clean, soft look to the interiors. Bleached oak floors and cabinets contrast with graying salvaged cypress outside on shutters, railings, and handrails.

Santa Barbara design codes required stucco siding, recessed windows, and red tile roofs at Yanonali Court. *Photo courtesy of Jeffrey Berkus Architects*

The cool roofs hint at more smart green features inside homes. A host of measures such as spray foam insulation, long-lasting materials, and energy-efficient appliances help to conserve water and energy and increase durability. In fact, all homes are required to be third-party-certified as green homes by the Florida Green Building Coalition, making Alys Beach the first community in Florida to do so. "These days it's not that difficult to be green," says Khoury. "Maybe before you used to have to make compromises, but these days there's no excuse."

CITY ORDINANCES SOMETIMES DICTATE HOME DESIGNS. The city of Santa Barbara, for instance, has one of the most restrictive design codes in the country. It requires that homes within certain older districts be composed with white stucco, recessed windows, and red-tile-roofs in the so-called Santa Barbara style. Popularized by local architect George Washington Smith, the city adopted this style during its rebuilding efforts after a 1925 earthquake. Smith's better work, in addition to predictable white stucco walls and red tile roofs, emphasized unique iron work, loggias that doubled as sleeping porches, and rooms accessed only through outdoor staircases.

For years, the Santa-Barbara-based Berkus Design Group, which was known throughout the country for contemporary home design, chafed under the prescriptive criteria. But sometimes the friction produced great results, like the five-home condominium, Yanonali Court, in downtown Santa Barbara. The homes, built on the quarter-acre site of a former hotel and apartment building, range from a 900-square-foot, one-bedroom to a 2,000-square-foot three-bedroom. The project fell within the city's Spanish colonial district, with an overlay that required a 1930s context. The city required that the homes surround a central courtyard. Jeffrey Berkus, working from preliminary plans done by his father Barry, had some fun with the courtyard. He made room for an outdoor fireplace and a fountain. "The courtyard incorporates all the natural elements—earth, air, water, and fire," he says.

The buildings, with their crisp stucco walls, setback windows, and red tile roofs, respect a local architectural tradition that blends Spanish, Mediterranean, and Moorish influences. But Berkus included an eclectic mix

Each element—earth, water, fire, air—finds a place in a shared courtyard at the heart of the condominium project. *Photo courtesy of Jeffrey Berkus Architects*

A lit art niche, wrought-iron railings, and dark wood accents give the interiors a clean, Spanish-inspired appearance. *Photo courtesy of Jeffrey Berkus Architects*

The community layout provides each home with a private courtyard and terrace. Some homes even have a roof deck. *Photo courtesy of Jeffrey Berkus Architects*

of details—custom wrought iron railings, tiled staircases, short columns, and sculpted railings—that gives the community its own personality. Bump-outs, recessed windows, and dark eaves create architectural rhythm. Dark downspouts break down stucco masses into manageable pieces. The defining detail—a wood-paneled bay window—hangs out over the courtyard. "You see the corner bay window on some of George Washington Smith's work," says Berkus.

The five homes go together like a Rubik's cube, arranged to give each a private, unique arrival sequence. Some owners enter at ground level, others from stairways. Each home has a private courtyard; some have a roof deck. Carefully positioned windows, terraces, balconies, and decks look out over the community and the surrounding neighborhood of apartments and single-family homes. Outdoor spaces and windows light the interiors from at least two, usually three, and sometimes even four directions. Windows and doors are set deep within the walls to avoid high-afternoon sunshine.

The traditional project is thoroughly modern from a tech perspective. One of the first LEED Platinum projects in the country, it served as a model for Santa Barbara's green building program. A cistern collects rainwater from the roof, using it to water the landscape, though native and Mediterranean plants require minimal irrigation. Pervious pavers percolate rainwater into the ground rather than direct it to the city's sewers.

SOMETIMES THE DESIGN PROGRAM FOR A HOME STEMS FROM THE SIMPLE DESIRE TO FIT INTO THE NEIGHBORHOOD. That was the case with a Richard Williams commission in Garrett Park, Maryland. After the previous home on the lot, a Victorian, burned beyond repair, government officials initially hoped it would be rebuilt in a similar style. In his design for a modern farmhouse, Williams picked up on familiar neighborhood elements—a gabled roof, a spacious front porch, and lap siding. But he stopped short of creating a completely nostalgic façade, contrasting wood-trimmed windows with pale cedar walls and playing with forms. What looks like a chimney rising above the roof is actually a light well for the stair hall. An unusual wall of square windows occupies one corner of the home. No-nonsense columns support the porch.

Architects often serve as marriage counselors, trying to find design solutions that reconcile differences. In this case, the wife preferred traditional design while the husband wanted something more contemporary. Williams split the difference with a transitional exterior coupled with a more modern, open floor plan. Upon entry, visitors look right through tall hallway windows to a reflecting pool and a modern garden. The living and dining rooms in between merge due to a common palette of warm, natural, sustainable materials. "You open the door and say, 'Wow, this isn't Kansas anymore,'" he says. As beautiful as the interiors are, Williams likes to think of the house as a connection, not an object—the bridge to a wonderful landscape plan done by Gregg Bleam of Charlottesville, Virginia.

Williams pushed the home to the edge of the lot to maximize backyard views from the house. The floor plan takes an L-shape—with the wide portion in front and the short line bounding the garden. Spare native plantings in the backyard—hornbeam trees frame a large lawn with a single Jane magnolia—make it a quiet, tranquil spot. A shallow reflecting pond, its planter filled with horsetail, sits close to the house. A banquette next to a large corner window provides the ideal spot to contemplate the pond. "The idea is to have a picnic next to the water," says Williams.

Minimal interior details don't detract attention from the view. Oak floors, a masonry fireplace, and a wood-paneled ceiling in the dining area warm the contemporary interiors. Lighter finishes contrast with dark limestone. The open plan includes an escape room—separated from the great room by a sliding barn door—to read a book, play an instrument, or get some work done. The addition of a day bed makes it an ideal place to park a visiting grandchild. The first-floor guest suite could one day become a master bedroom, if managing the stairs becomes a problem.

The boomer couple wanted this to be their last home. Williams left room behind a wall for an elevator shaft in case the couple wanted to run one to their current master bedroom on the second floor. He designed a low-threshold side entrance to a wide hallway for wheelchair accessibility. An office above the garage could be converted to a caretaker's suite if the couple needed in-home help. It also serves as insurance against a child who returns to the roost. The overarching idea was to design a house with rooms that the couple would use on most days. But these same rooms could morph into bedrooms for visits by grown children and grandchildren.

The couple decided to spend money now on energy efficient features that will hold down utility bills later, when their income may be limited. The house employs a geothermal heating and cooling system, foam insulation, and an insulated aluminum roof. The package of energy details was enough to earn the home a LEED Silver certification from the US Green Building Council, something else that homeowners long ago—or even fifteen years ago—never considered.

6.
CONTAIN MODERN ELEMENTS

THE NEW MODERN IS WARM, NOT STERILE

A movement has swept the housing market since the economic crash of 2008—the rise of modern architecture within reach of mainstream homebuyers. These aren't the glass and steel homes done after WWII designed to emphasize the miracle of industrial design. Nor are they the sterile lofts depicted in *Elle Decor* during the 1990s, the ones where the only color against a white backdrop was a husband dressed in black, inertly reading an art book. Today's modern homes are likely to be warmer—thanks to the incorporation of wood and stone—with far more attention paid to comfort, privacy, and livability. They don't expose every movement to neighborhood scrutiny. But they do work overtime to capture exterior views.

The rise of modern home design is a big change from the two decades that led up to the housing boom when architects, catering to overworked baby boomers yearning for simpler times, imported nostalgic styles and details from Europe. They journeyed to Italy and Spain to study eave and roof details and courtyard design. They responded to market research that indicated that hard-working baby boomers wanted traditional designs that reminded them of more peaceful times. By 2008, when the market went to hell in a handbasket, leaving legions of traditionally styled homes sitting unsold in subdivisions across America, it was time for something different.

A new and slightly different American Dream of homeownership seems to have surfaced. A new generation of homeowners that never visited their great grandparents' home seems drawn to simple, clean, elegant design. They prefer to look forward rather than backward to a history that wasn't theirs. These new aspirations are mirrored in television commercials for cars shot in front of iconic contemporary homes. Couples discuss financial matters from Eames chairs looking out huge picture windows. Architect Mike Woodley, who designs homes for builders and homeowners, says most builder clients prefer to go the safe route and design traditional homes that they think stand a better chance of selling. But when he deals directly with homeowners, they want a more contemporary home. "When people don't have a builder telling them what they want, this is invariably what they do," he says.

MODERN HOMES OFTEN DELIVER THE UNEXPECTED. Todd Walker's Hannah's House, for instance, plays delightful games with the eyes. The garage to the 3,040-square-foot modern farmhouse, named by the architect after his then-young daughter, appears asymmetrical, until you realize that the roof isn't centered over the middle. The large resulting eave covers a porch. One front wall, angled cartoonishly inward, keeps unwanted summer sun out of the house. The front porch looks pretty traditional, but it's slightly askew. Roof overhangs range from a seemingly random two to six feet, until you learn that each length is carefully calculated to protect the house from the sun year-round.

This was another of those homes, located in the Harbor Town community in Memphis, Tennessee, that the jury just loved—it's quirky, modern, sociable, and affordable. The principal of archimania relied on a bevy of unusual materials—

concrete block (split-faced on the back of the home, smooth inside), pipe columns, birch veneer plywood, and maple flooring. But the materials are also affordable; he brought in the home for only $90 a square foot, excluding land, a great price for a custom home. The budget included ten-inch shiplap redwood used for bottom siding courses to give the building depth. Less-expensive six-inch strips of fiber-cement siding top it.

Material savings went to execute architectural details. A whimsical tower, reminiscent of the lookouts that used to dot the Mississippi River shoreline, houses Walker's office. The tower, accessed via a ship ladder, cantilevers over the rear of a steeply sloping lot. Walker can watch boat traffic on the river and trucks that come and go from an industrial warehouse area on the opposite bank.

In the family room, a red window wall of asymmetrical shapes, made from an aluminum storefront system, looks out over the neighborhood walking path. The windows turn black at night for privacy, though a steep lot grade prevents passersby from seeing much inside anyway. The family room is turned at a slight angle so that Walker and his wife could watch Hannah and her friends play on the lawn outside. Each first-floor window seems to have its own story; it may be positioned to capture a specific view, control privacy, or provide natural light.

The house is both inventive and pragmatic. It's long on built-in storage, a major hot button for any growing family. When visitors arrive, the Walkers can quickly stash toys, games, and blankets in a large storage unit tucked under

the window wall. Cubbyholes in the bedroom closets and kitchen are ideal for storing shoes, clothes, cookbooks, and even small dishes. Built-in alcoves on each side of the master bed serve as repositories for books, alarm clocks, slippers, and anything else you want to hide from sight. Usefulness is the focus of the master bath. It has built-in hampers, cubbies, and a make-up station. Throughout, bright colors, warm woods, and strong accents prove that modern homes are anything but sterile.

IF MODERN HOME DESIGN INCORPORATES THE LATEST TECHNOLOGY, it also makes the most of the natural environment. In the case of Marsh House, Mark McInturff's client, builder Patty McDaniel, wanted a modern design with a big back porch to look out over a marsh near Rehoboth Bay in Delaware. McDaniel managed to secure a lot that butts up against the wetlands bordering Rehoboth Bay. A canal runs a little more than 1,000 feet from the site. McInturff, the principal of McInturff Architects, delivered a minimalist design that makes the most of stunning vistas of the marsh, water, and sky.

McDaniel could only build on solid land as required by the US Army Corps of Engineers. The home's foundation carefully follows the contours of solid ground where the wetlands end. The outline results in an irregular form—three walls are straight but a fourth (the one with the back porch) bends with the line of the wetlands. McInturff describes the form as an open book, with a spine rising from the corner to show off the splayed pages—a two-story porch built with tropical hardwood and galvanized steel. Interior balconies from second-floor rooms look out over the porch. It's almost as though the architect designed a porch with a house attached.

An interior balcony overlooks a
two-story porch supported by a
metal frame that showcases the
builder's skill. *Photo by Julia Heine*

White walls, neutral grays, and
minimal trim transfer attention to
the outdoors. *Photo by Julia Heine*

McInturff strives to design homes that make "a strong statement at entry. The best homes have a big moment when the design of the house is revealed," he says. Opening the front door reveals a view of the marsh through large, undivided windows and the two-story screened porch. An open floor plan and neutral interior palette focus attention on the killer views. The home's lateral bracing and structural steel, important when building this close to the ocean, is left exposed so that visitors can appreciate McDaniel's craft. She spends lots of time on the porch and on calm mornings can sometimes hear waves hitting the beach a mile and a half away. During summers, she can watch herons fish the marsh and ospreys occupy nesting platforms. At night, fox and deer come out.

The main floor, which is actually the second floor, contains most rooms that McDaniel needs on a daily basis, including a master bedroom. A loft and a couple of bedrooms for family visitors, each with a terrace to the screened porch, comprise the third floor. Windows in the second-story hallway look through the porch to the marsh. Two walls to the guest bedroom are almost all glass to capture the views. A metal ladder hanging on the wall of the second-story landing leads to a hatch that opens to a walled observation area on the flat roof.

White walls, with limited trim details, contrast with dark brown cork flooring downstairs and gray carpet upstairs. McInturff hid light switches on the side of the kitchen island to keep them off the walls. The kitchen cabinetry, which extends into the hallway to create a pantry, matches the wood used to make the dining table. Most living room furniture was kept a neutral gray.

In the modernist tradition, the home's white walls leave room for self-expression. But McDaniel likes the aesthetic so much, and the focus on water views, that she isn't sure whether she wants to clutter the walls with art.

7.
CATER TO HUMAN OCCUPANTS

THE BEST HOMES PROVIDE APPROPRIATE CREATURE COMFORTS

CARSON LOONEY LIKES TO SWEAT THE SMALL STUFF, drawing details down to tie racks, garage walls that won't dent, and bunk beds. He pays particularly close attention to the spaces that get used the most, especially the great room, kitchen, and master bedroom suite. These also happen to be the rooms most likely to get blown out of proportion in McMansions. Even in the biggest custom homes, he draws key rooms to a comfortable human scale, visualizing how the rooms are likely to be used. "That's how you create the impression that, wow, I could actually live here," he says.

The architect's passion for human scale is very much on display in a custom home he designed in a close-in Memphis suburb. The great room might have been twice as big in another architect's hands. In this home, it's a comfortable place to watch a game and converse with a cook in the kitchen. The television is set at eye level rather than elevated over the fireplace where it's hard to watch—one of Looney's pet peeves. Remotely controlled drapes make it easy to adjust lighting for the big game or movie, and built-in speakers broadcast full sound into every corner. The great room, Looney firmly believes, is the one space that everyone wants, regardless of means. "If you had this and a couple of bedrooms, you'd be all set," he says.

Some real estate agents might complain about the modest scale of the kitchen in a home this size. "Where are the second oven, warming drawer, and extra cabinet space, they may ask. But all those accoutrements don't have to be in the main kitchen space," he says. "If you put them in a pantry, you can use open shelving or a cheaper grade of cabinetry."

The outdoor room is the latest object of Looney's passion. But it's likely to be little more than window dressing unless it's comfortable to use almost year-round. In the Memphis home, heaters in the floor and ceiling, coupled with a large hearth bordered by shelves for log storage, warm the space on cold days. A covered ceiling with fans provides cooling during hot summer months.

By the same token, the owners could have afforded an elaborate front façade—a more conspicuous demonstration of their wealth. They opted instead for a simple roofline and an entry that brings the elegant materials used on the home down to hand and eye level. The savings in scale left room for tasteful, natural materials—stone corbels and timber crossheads, which the architect arranged to great effect. Each element serves a structural purpose. No showy extras were tacked on. "Simple translates into elegant virtually every time," says Looney.

Looney prefers that homes reveal themselves in stages, a technique he jokingly says he borrowed from tasteful strippers in the 1920s. The front entry hall in the Memphis house is still grand at eleven feet tall. But what catches your eye is the focused view through the foyer to windows that look out on the beautifully appointed outdoor room. "People don't look up as much as they look out the window," he says. "That view is more important than hanging a chandelier twenty feet in the air."

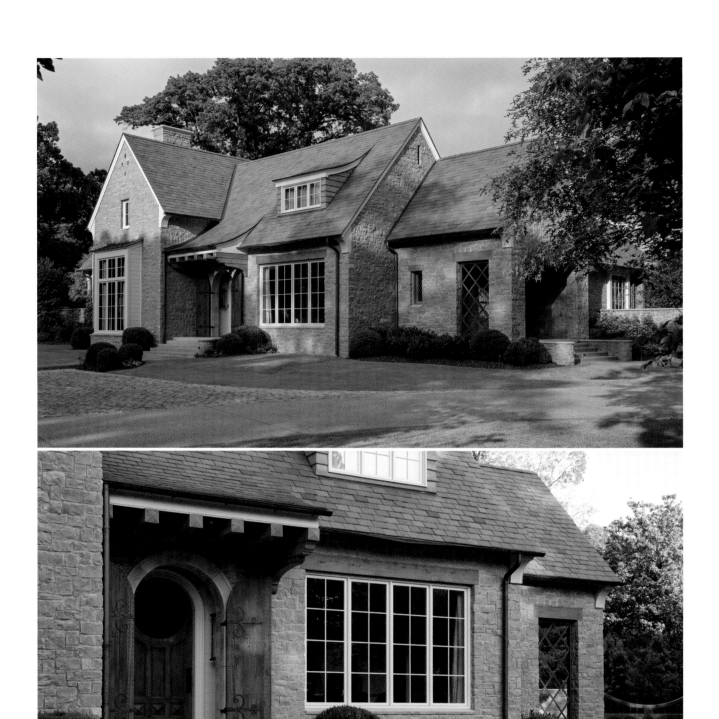

The foyer leads to a long hallway that covers the width of the home. So-called gallery plans work great for people who want to showcase art and collectibles. But hallways can be less than inviting without a focal point at the end. In this case, the view is a perfectly centered, light-filled window. A great piece of furniture or an art niche also works as a focal point, especially if it is lit. "That's one of those things that makes people say, I don't know what it is, but it feels good," says Looney.

Looney applies the same less-is-more discipline to master bedrooms suites. They are often oversized in custom homes, to the point where they aren't practical. He lowered the shower ceiling in this home to create a cocoon-like environment that heats quickly on a cold winter morning. "All these builders out West are doing these crazy walk-through showers with glass walls," Looney says. "I call them car wash showers. You have to clean them. They are cold in the morning. People like them when they see them in a model home, but they hate them when they use them. Taking a shower is one of the most important functions in a home."

This master bath includes the requisite dual lavatories, one for beard hair and the occasional toothpaste dollop. But there's also space to store a hairdryer and medicine. The toilet is compartmentalized behind a door for privacy, with a window "that helps the digestive system. We left being cave men long ago." The space is noteworthy for what it doesn't include, such as a make-up desk with a television behind the mirror, or a table and subdued lighting for in-home massages. A view from the bathroom to a small outdoor courtyard—an ideal spot to stretch or soak up morning sun—makes the modest bathroom read larger and helps create a spa-like atmosphere.

Master bedroom sizes came roaring back as the housing market recovered in the mid-2010s. Many vestiges from the housing boom—sitting rooms, coffee bars, and entertainment centers—have returned. Looney is convinced that, no matter how big its size, people don't spend too much time in the master bedroom. If the room gets too big, it may be difficult to watch TV on the wall opposite the bed or to navigate your way to the toilet at night. He leaves enough room for a chair on which to read a book or tie shoelaces. But he rarely includes a sitting room, even in the largest customs, partly because those homes typically include a study, home office, and other private space.

Instead, Looney concentrates on useful storage. A closet in the hallway leading into the master bedroom is an ideal spot to stow luggage. The walk-in master closet includes specialty racks for ties and belts and a drawer for underwear, all within easy reach. "It's ergonomically designed, like you'd see in a car," he says. Though the built-ins in this home are real wood, the same level of organization would be achieved with inexpensive painted gypsum and pressed boards. "No one has ever said they have enough storage. But I've had many people say, if I had it to do over, I wouldn't make that room so large and I'd add more storage," Looney says.

Homebuyer surveys consistently show that people wish their new home had more storage—of all kinds. Knowing this, design juries often salute specialized storage spaces, especially when it shows up in unexpected places. They reward space carved out of the garage for a workshop, fishing closet, golf storage, or dog washing. They admire kitchens with shelves for cookbooks and hooks over cooktops for pots and pans. They salute "Texas basements"—storage space carved out of the attic in places where shifting soils makes basement construction impractical.

A long central hallway culminating in a light-filled view provides access to most first-floor rooms. *Photo by Jack Gardner*

Looney resisted the temptation to oversize the kitchen, putting a second prep kitchen around the corner. *Photo by Jack Gardner*

PLANS / The home centers around a great room and long navigational corridor. *Diagrams courtesy of LRK*

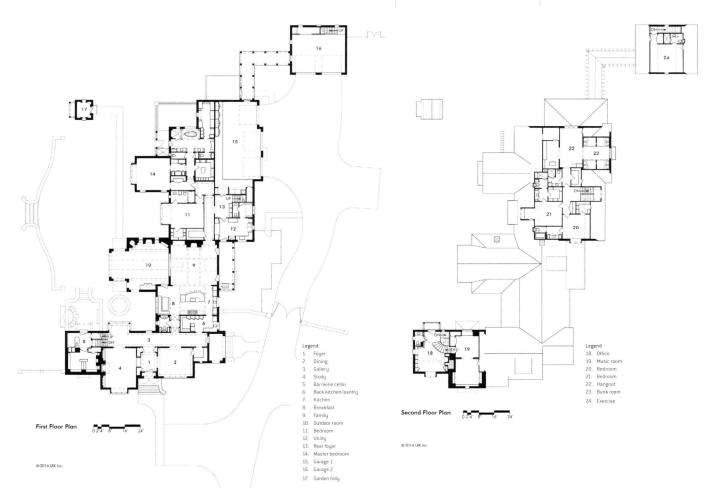

First Floor Plan   0 2'4' 8'   16'   24'

©2016 LRK Inc.

Second Floor Plan   0 2'4' 8'   16'   24'

©2016 LRK Inc.

Legend
1. Foyer
2. Dining
3. Gallery
4. Study
5. Bar/wine cellar
6. Back kitchen/pantry
7. Kitchen
8. Breakfast
9. Family
10. Outdoor room
11. Bedroom
12. Utility
13. Rear foyer
14. Master bedroom
15. Garage 1
16. Garage 2
17. Garden folly

Legend
18. Office
19. Music room
20. Bedroom
21. Bedroom
22. Hangout
23. Bunk room
24. Exercise

Looney pioneered a more mundane storage space often found in new homes today: the mudroom. He refers to the space as a "liver" since it filters impurities before they enter the house. A basic mudroom may have hooks for coats and backpacks, cubbies for lunch boxes, maybe even in a bench for taking off shoes. "But you need to think through all the goings and comings of daily life for everyone in the house, in the same way you think of all the things you want to do in the kitchen," Looney says. "Every night I bring in my briefcase and many times I have plans. Where do those go? What about other members of the family? Maybe they bring home hockey equipment or dry cleaning that they don't want to drag through the house."

Looney's latest preoccupation is with something else that's commonly overlooked—pets. More than half of American families have them, yet most new homes don't have designated places to feed, wash, and leash them. The owners of the Memphis house had an even more complicated situation—two dogs, one big, one little. Looney explains: "They didn't want the big dog to eat the little dog's food. We designed a low cabinet module in the laundry room for the little dog. The big dog won't be able to get down that low." When guests come over, the dogs are sequestered to a laundry room with a Dutch door. The upper portion can be left open so that the dogs don't feel completely left out.

A big fireplace and heaters in the floor and ceiling make this outdoor room comfortable for year-round use. *Photo by Jack Gardner*

The children's playroom over the garage includes built-in bunks for a sleepover party. *Photo by Jack Gardner*

The master bath combines romance (a pearl-shaped tub) with practicality (storage within easy reach). *Photo by Jack Gardner*

Another issue that bedevils architects and homebuyers alike is the appropriate size of secondary bedrooms. In some spec homes, particularly in Southern California and the Southwest, where people spend so much time outside, secondary bedrooms may get really small, no bigger than eight-and-a-half feet by ten feet. At that size, assuming you don't want to block the window with furniture, you'd better know where the bed, dresser, and nightstand are going. There may not be room for much else, not even a desk to do homework. Though he can make even the smallest bedroom work, Looney prefers something along the lines of twelve by thirteen feet. "It's a nice size; it works for carpet," he says. "My children's bedrooms were that size. It leaves room for a small desk, a dresser, and maybe a little side chair. A queen-sized bed fits. You aren't bumping into everything. I have so many clients who think a kid's bedroom needs to be fifteen by thirteen. Geez, we do masters that size."

Easy-to-build forms and inexpensive materials contained the construction cost of House in the Woods by Todd Walker. *Photo by Jeffrey Jacobs*

THE MOST SUCCESSFUL HOMES DELIVER GREAT SPACES WHERE FAMILIES CAN SPEND TIME TOGETHER. In the case of a home on seven wooded acres that Todd Walker designed for a family that wanted a quality place to raise children, it was a double-height screened porch. Walker sited the porch—which he compares to an inexpensive "lean-to"—to absorb plenty of daytime sunlight, enough that it can be used nearly year-round. "It's essentially their family room. It's as big as a two-car garage. They cook and eat out there. They essentially live in the woods," Walker says.

The same might be said of the main house, lit by an expansive two-story wall with an unusual window pattern. A suspended second-floor hallway, set back from the window wall, creates an atrium effect in the main living areas. Walker stacked living, dining, and cooking spaces back to back in the floor plan. Joined by a long hallway and separated by short walls, they borrow space from each other. A simple kitchen with a four-seat island is tied together with flush cabinets, black counters and appliances, and stainless steel hardware. Pendant lighting hangs close to kitchen work surfaces.

"People may look at the two-dimensional plan and say, 'that's nothing special.' But the ultimate test is how the plan is articulated in three dimensions," Walker says. "Spaces may have special volumes and details. There may be more than one use for a room, and rooms often borrow space from each other."

Walker detached the garage from the house because of the owner's unusual hobby—rebuilding and restoring cars. Separating the garage prevents much of the sound of sawing metal from reaching the main house. As an added precaution, an extra layer of insulation was added to the closest wall of the main house.

On the exterior, a combination of vertical and horizontal siding patterns, along with a simple gabled roof, reference nearby rural buildings, as do the ventilation slats below the soffits. "We sort of used it as a louvered system, reminiscent of old agrarian buildings, like a corn crib or ventilated barn," Walker says. The main house, clad with corrugated metal and concrete board slats, mirrors the mass and scale of a log home on the adjoining property. The collection of simple forms, coupled with inexpensive materials, kept the budget to less than $100 per square foot. The home is a simple solution to rural housing, a nice alternative to "off the shelf" ranch style homes commonly found in this neck of the woods.

A two-story window wall, with second-floor stairs set back to create an atrium, lends drama to interior spaces. *Photo by Jeffrey Jacobs*

With everything within easy reach, this simple kitchen works well for a small family. *Photo by Jeffrey Jacobs*

The family spends most days on a large screened porch that feels like part of the surrounding woods. *Photo by Jeffrey Jacobs*

"One thing we try to do is find beauty in simplicity," Walker says. "Often people spend a lot of money and they just create chaos. We find the use of materials sets the tone for the project budget. If you have an elaborate material that takes a refined detail, that's going to take up a big part of the budget. The material not only costs more, but so does the labor."

Strategic use of detailing allows Walker to concentrate on features that improve quality of life at home in the long run, whether it's a detached garage, pool house, or even an observatory. A good architect can translate dreams and aspirations into very real blueprints. But a key part of that exercise is figuring out in advance what you really want in your next home.

8.
MAKE ECONOMICAL
USE OF SPACE

THE BEST HOMES FIND A USE—OR TWO—FOR EVERY SQUARE FOOT

Most people appreciate a great restaurant meal, creatively prepared with fresh ingredients, maybe even ones procured directly from a farm. They value quality over quantity, in other words. The best home designs work in much the same way. Skilled architects can create a much more appetizing home when they focus on quality living space rather than quantity of square footage. Square footage can easily be reduced by twenty to thirty percent by thoroughly analyzing how space will be used, borrowing space from other rooms, and opening outdoor views that make interiors look larger.

This approach won't work, though, without a good idea of what you want in a home, a process that begins by thinking about key at-home activities. Do you spend gobs of time watching television as a family, grill three times a week outside, entertain neighbors every weekend, spend most evenings reading novels, practice every weekend with a rock band? Where do you prefer to do these things? The answers may provide a clear picture of the home you covet.

Most architects begin the design process with a thorough client interview. San Francisco architect Steven House used to interview clients in person, until he realized that one partner usually dominated the conversation. Now he asks both partners to independently complete a very detailed survey that includes some personal questions, like "What happens after a bad argument? Where do you go to make up?" He keeps the findings by his side as he designs a shared dream home.

Most homeowners who build a new home today desire an open floor plan that combines living, cooking, entertainment, and eating spaces. The approach cuts down on interior walls and seldom-used rooms right from the gate, creating a more space-efficient home. In the best open plans, ceiling, wall, and floor treatments define activity zones. This may be as simple as varying floor coverings, ceiling heights, or trim details to designate a television viewing space or a dining nook. Dropping the ceiling over the oven or kitchen island not only defines the space but also brings task lighting and air handling closer to where it's needed. Raising the kitchen counter closest to the family room hides messy dishes from visitors.

The big question for most people is whether to dispense with a formal living and dining room. The Eisenhower generation prized the living room as a place to sip a Gibson, smoke Lucky Strikes, tell stories about family history, and gaze at picture books. My grandmother passed down a living room table with all the battle scars—burn marks, ring marks, and wood blemishes—of a party veteran. When younger generations throw a party, it usually starts in the kitchen, then migrates to another casual space, if it moves at all. We designed a show home for young homeowners one year with a driveway courtyard that included a beer pong table. No formal living room or dining room, just a small family room and a flex room for Pilates or playing with children.

Other rooms you think you need—maybe to improve the resale value of your home—may prove unnecessary. You may believe you need a guest room and rationalize it as a way to maximize bedroom count. But unless guests visit frequently, you might be better off with a more flexible space where you can do the things you love—like ride a stationary bike or write a blog. Frank Lloyd Wright often designed offices with built-in daybeds to nap or sleep a guest. With space for a closet and a window for egress, the room still qualifies as a bedroom.

A built-in banquette saves floor space while providing a welcoming seating area, and stools tuck neatly under the cantilevered island counter. JZMK Partners. *Photo by Eric Hernandez*

At Pinehills, a deep wall at the top of the landing accommodates a built-in bookcase and a bench for tying shoes. *Photo courtesy of Pinehills*

These days people are even thinking twice about formal offices. Wireless networks mean that unless you are doing serious or noisy work at home that requires privacy—maybe you need to do engineering calculations or make sales over the phone—you can perch with a laptop in front of a big picture window. The key to enjoying a distributed work environment is having a strong Wi-Fi system. That means bringing as much bandwidth into the house as possible and installing an upgraded router (rather than the free one given to you by an Internet service provider). The best place to put it is a high spot where it can transmit signals like an umbrella over your house and property. The bottom line is, your money may be better spent on a great porch or patio than a home office.

Even so, many open plans come with an "away" room on the main floor, a sanctuary to escape from household noise and activity. It could be as simple as creating a parlor by the main entry; with French doors, it could double as a music room. Several homes featured in this book skillfully integrate away rooms, separated by sliding barn doors, into main living areas. The beauty of that approach is that when no one else is home, you can open the doors and enjoy the view or breezes through the great room. When you need quiet, you can close the doors. The cost of sliding barn doors, and the hardware that suspends them, has fallen to the point where it's a very common spec.

If you absolutely require a dining room, maybe it could include built-in shelving, a comfortable chair in the corner, or a pullout desk to pay the bills. The dining room could double as a library with the addition of bookshelves along the walls. A chandelier hung low over the table could make it the ultimate homework spot. One of our kids preferred doing homework in the solitude of his room. The other one wanted to do it anywhere but his room. He also preferred being on a ball field to being at home.

A butted glass window designed by Kevin deFreitas makes the corner of the room disappear, focusing attention on the trees outside. *Photo by Darren Bradley*

Speaking of which, I've never understood why builder spec homes don't do a better job of accommodating home sports. The occasional exercise room is about all you see. We twice built show homes with garages that doubled as indoor basketball courts. The key was having enough roof clearance, a minimum of twenty feet, to shoot a high-arcing jumper. A Home of the Future show home we built in a Dallas suburb in 1997 included a tennis practice facility in the garage, a feature inspired by a neighbor when I was young. Dr. Utiger used to open the garage door on Saturday morning, put the car in the street, and slam tennis balls against the reinforced back wall of the garage for hours at a time.

Another option is to dedicate space in or near the large master bedroom to a small nursery. This isn't a new idea—my great grandfather did it in a Phoenix estate he built in the 1920s. When I visited more than eighty years later, the nursery had been converted into a large walk-in closet. (The home still had its original dumbwaiter to serve second-floor porch parties, an elevator for elderly guests, and a secret passage to escape to the pool area in case someone nasty came knocking at the door.) Frank Lloyd Wright included a nursery adjacent to the master bedroom in his Hyde Park Chicago home. His wife nursed their children in a low-ceilinged alcove by the window. Spaces like this can be recaptured for other uses later on—like watching television, enjoying coffee or wine, or storing clothes.

One of the more subtle space-saving techniques is to "dissolve" the corners of rooms—borrow visual space from adjoining rooms by not fully enclosing them. When you can see part of an office or library from the great room, it makes the great room, and the house, appear larger. The effect is magnified when these views are visible from the places where you spend the most time, like the kitchen or great room.

A playful interior window separates the dining space, making this narrow apartment seem larger.
Photo courtesy of Lander Group

Another secret to effective small-home design: don't waste space on circulation. This is an area where production builders, watching every penny spent on square footage, often excel. I'll never forget an afternoon spent in San Antonio walking a series of three-bedroom, one-story affordable demonstration homes, most of them less than 1,200 square feet. What you noticed immediately was a lack of hallway space and interior walls in the best plans. Entry foyers opened to great rooms, sometimes with a half-wall separating dining from living space. You often entered the master directly from the great room, but the builder made sure you couldn't see into the bedroom from the entry. A short hallway led to two additional bedrooms and a shared bathroom. Washers and dryers were stacked in a closet.

When circulation space is inevitable, it can serve multiple purposes. Widening hallways by only one foot leaves enough room for built-in shelving to hold books, mementos, and artwork. Architect Ross Chapin, principal of Ross Chapin Architects, renown for his cottage designs, looks for opportunities to add a windowed alcove on a stair landing. It's an ideal spot to curl up with an e-reader, take a nap, or even sleep a grandchild.

Making the most of vertical space is a classic technique for saving on floor area. Bunk beds, a staple of beach houses, may be the most time-honored solution. Putting upper cabinets in the pantry or utility rooms for bulk storage, rarely used appliances, and holiday decorations is another classic example. Tall shelves in the garage for weed

THE KEY TO SPACE-EFFICIENT INTERIORS: VISUALIZE SPACES IN THREE DIMENSIONS. Jim Zack put those skills to work in his design for Steel House, two small townhomes on a narrow but deep San Francisco lot where only one home had stood before. The first challenge was how to subdivide the lot so that both 1,500-square-foot homes would feel private and draw light. He decided to place the homes back to back, separated by a courtyard. A front walk goes around the side of the home in front, leading to the shared green space.

The centerpiece of the three-story home in front is one of Zack's signature staircases. Composed with steel stringers, acrylic risers, and glass walls, the stairs appear to float, and the stairwell functions as a source of secondary light for the main living spaces. It also provides access to copious shelving. In the kitchen, frosted glass on the bottom portion of floor-to-ceiling windows provides privacy; the frosted portion lines up with low privacy walls in the family room.

A steel beam visually separates the living room from the kitchen and dining spaces. Oiled-oak floors and custom walnut cabinetry warm the interiors. A small desk recessed into a wall of kitchen cabinets provides the perfect place to conduct family business. Upstairs on the bedroom level, a bookcase wall divides the master bedroom from a living area. Open shelves—an extension of the staircase bookshelves—serve the upper level. A private roof deck off the master bedroom looks west to the sunset, making it an ideal cocktail hour spot.

An open stairwell ushers light into the house on the back half of the lot. *Photo by Zack|de Vito Architecture and Bruce Damonte*

The two homes meet in an internal courtyard, zoned to create private spaces. *Photo by Zack|de Vito Architecture and Bruce Damonte*

A built-in bookshelf wall separates sleep from study in a thoughtful master bedroom retreat. *Photo by Zack|de Vito Architecture and Bruce Damonte*

PLANS / The bigger home in front enjoys privacy from the street. The home in back sports a balcony to the rear. *Photo by Zack|de Vito Architecture and Bruce Damonte*

1. entry
2. courtyard
3. garage
4. bedroom
5. study/office
6. walk-in wardrobe
7. bathroom
8. laundry
9. mechanical room
10. kitchen
11. living room
12. dining room
13. patio/balcony

Floor Plans

N

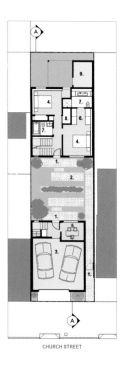

GROUND LEVEL

2ND FLOOR

3RD FLOOR

A first-floor office, with a patio door that could be left open on warm days, faces the shared garden courtyard. Business visitors could use a small gate to one side of the house without disturbing the rest of the household. Because of its relative privacy, the room could be used as a guest bedroom, though guests would have to climb stairs to use a bathroom. The office shares the lower level with parking for two cars, with one space for the resident of the home on the back half of the lot.

The interior courtyard brings light to the second home, only two stories tall. Zack moved the main public rooms, along with the master suite, to the second floor where the views are better, producing an upside-down house, as it's known in the trade. He put two bedrooms and baths on the lower level. Upstairs, the kitchen and master bedroom access a private deck that faces southwest, away from the house in front. Once again the staircase, built into the first-floor walls, is a work of art; its walnut risers and treads blend with bookshelves and an oiled-oak floor. Elsewhere, brightly colored doors stand out against an otherwise neutral color scheme of browns, whites, and black. Custom rift-cut white oak cabinetry and composite quartz countertops highlight a top-drawer kitchen design.

The Lyon Park House by Robert Gurney respects the scale and rhythm of a largely colonial streetscape even as it forges a singular identity. *Photo by Anice Hoachlander*

A major reworking of a compartmentalized floor plan results in more useful space with floor-to-ceiling views of a backyard garden. *Photo by Anice Hoachlander*

MAKING BETTER USE OF SPACE IS OFTEN THE PRIME MOVER BEHIND REMODELING PROJECTS. That was the case with the Lyon Park House by Robert Gurney Architect for an Arlington, Virginia, family. After seven years of living in a cramped colonial, the four-member Timura Frasier household decided it was time for a change, if not a radical break. The family had outgrown their two-bedroom, one-bath, 1,400-square foot home. It contained a series of small, unconnected rooms, and a stairwell bisected the house, reducing livable space and limiting sight lines. A pitched roof made the upstairs bedrooms feel small. The owners longed for a more contemporary, light-filled home with an open floor plan that would take advantage of a wonderful sloping lot full of old trees.

Gurney completely reconfigured the home's internal circulation. He replaced the second-story walls, raised the roof, and relocated the stairs to an addition on one side. Those moves added 400 square feet to the second floor, which now houses four bedrooms and two bathrooms. The master has its own bathroom; the three other bedrooms, one used as an office, share a hall bath. Raising the ceiling provided room for more glass that lets in more daylight, making the bedrooms much more appealing during the day.

Moving the stairwell and taking down interior walls allowed Gurney to create a long, diagonal view across the house. It culminates in floor-to-ceiling windows with expansive backyard views. Large windows facing the street connect to the neighborhood and fill the dining space with light. A large kitchen island anchors the family space. A built-in dishwasher and refrigerator create a consistent look in the kitchen. Wall ovens were moved to an outside wall and close to a window for venting.

The 2,100-square-foot home (excluding the basement) balances sustainability against the family budget. All the wood in the home, including five-and-a-quarter-inch sawn white oak flooring and the siding, was responsibly forested. Wood siding combines with gray stucco and charcoal fiber-cement panels to create a warm exterior that quietly recedes into the tree-lined streetscape. Despite its modern geometric appearance, the home's compact massing and simple fenestration respect the scale of adjacent houses. A rain screen system protects the exterior walls from rot, and high-efficiency windows minimize heat loss.

GROUND FLOOR PLAN *before*
0'   10'

GROUND FLOOR PLAN *after*
0'   10'

The design employs atypical but not overly expensive materials to make an impact. Polished concrete covers most of the first floor. White thermofoil cabinets and a man-made countertop material create a distinctive kitchen, even as they save money over solid-wood cabinets and quartz countertops. To economize without sacrificing style, the owners ordered stylish tile, light fixtures, and plumbing fittings directly from manufacturers over the Internet or from affordable local sources. They used distinctive, off-the-shelf vanities—raised off the floor—in lieu of custom ones.

Gurney's design anticipates storage, living, and furnishing needs to reduce clutter. Recessed lighting minimizes the need for lamps that might have interfered with views through the open first-floor plan. A sliding wood panel cabinet within

FIRST FLOOR PLAN *before*

0'   10'

FIRST FLOOR PLAN *after*

0'   10'

SECOND FLOOR PLAN *before*

0'   10'

SECOND FLOOR PLAN *after*

0'   10'

a stone media wall hides a television. A built-in armoire along an adjacent wall holds a storage cabinet and bookshelves for art and mementos. Convenient storage allows the space to be quickly converted from an active family room to entertaining space. Kalwall panels along one exterior wall provide natural light and privacy from neighbors.

The formerly forlorn basement is now a tempting, light-filled destination, complete with a family/entertainment room, wet bar, workshop that could be used as a guest bedroom, and full bathroom. Basement doors open to a patio perched over the sloping lot. All told, the renovation more than doubled living space, though it only marginally increased the home's footprint. This may be a modest project with a moderate budget, but the impact on the family of four was huge. It demonstrates how much better homes can live with rapt attention to how spaces will be used.

9.
PRACTICE
SUSTAINABILITY

With rooftop photovoltaic and hot water panels angled to optimize performance, the Glencoe House by Kipnis Architecture demonstrates that green homes don't have to be contemporary in design. *Photo courtesy Kipnis Architecture + Planning*

EVEN THE GREENEST HOUSE IS A NEGATIVE EVENT FOR THE ENVIRONMENT

Until recently, designers of sustainable homes strove to create buildings that produce as much energy as they consume. That's no longer good enough for some. The new high ground is a home that produces more energy than it requires. That way you can sell the excess power to the utility, reducing the negative environmental impact created by building even the most sustainable home. Laws in more than thirty-five states provide a big assist; they require utilities to buy electricity from homeowners at retail rates—the same rates that you pay when you buy electricity from the utility. State and federal tax breaks for buying energy-efficient equipment bring the net-positive goal within financial reach.

Even so, turning a home into a utility, per se, is fraught with peril. The finished home done by the unpracticed may not look good or live well. The biggest minefield: limiting windows to create the most energy-efficient building envelope possible may result in dark, drab living spaces. Another danger: overloading the home with expensive, hard-to-maintain equipment to save energy or water when simple architectural solutions could achieve the same outcome. If the home isn't designed to consume as little electricity as possible, it may need more solar panels than necessary to support it, and they are often the biggest expense.

THE FIRST ORDER OF BUSINESS WHEN DESIGNING A SUSTAINABLE HOME IS TO CONSIDER THE ORIENTATION of the sun on the lot. Chicago architect Nathan Kipnis always starts with a site study. He also needs to know whether he can take advantage of prevailing breezes or shade trees and how neighboring buildings will affect the home. Environmental factors were particularly important on a 2,800-square-foot home Kipnis Architecture + Planning designed for a couple that owns a coffee shop that had been called "the greenest in America." They wanted their house, dubbed Uncommon Ground, to receive similar accolades.

Standing in the way was the east-to-west orientation of a tight inner city Chicago lot. The back of the home would have to face west. The best situation is when the back of the home faces south. That way south-facing glass can be used to absorb solar heat during the winter when the sun is low in the sky. Porch overhangs, eaves, or window awnings can block sunlight during summer months when the sun is high in the sky. In the United States, the sun is always in the southern sky.

Complicating matters, only six feet would separate the house from its neighbors to the south and north. What few windows Kipnis put on those sides are above eye level to protect privacy. Most windows wound up on the east and west

Built on a snug inner-city lot, the
Uncommon Ground House relies
on a full menu of sustainable
techniques to overcome limited
opportunities for solar gain.
Photo by Wayne Cable

With natural ventilation, solar
panels, and energy-efficient
construction, the home produces
nearly all the power it needs.
Photo by Nate Kipnis

sides, where they can be a source of unwanted heat gain. Kipnis used window coatings to limit solar heat gain and allow visible light to pass. To make the home feel more open and airy, he designed a central skylight over a four-story stairwell. Light bounces off the stairwell walls, branching out into different floor levels. "It throws daylight all the way down to the basement," says Kipnis.

Natural ventilation minimizes air conditioning needs. Cool air enters through a series of stacked awning windows on the northeast side near the front door. "These can be opened up like a 'snake skin' to catch breezes coming from the north, east, or south," says Kipnis. Ceiling fans draw cool air from the basement and first floor, venting it through third-floor penthouse windows. "When you combine the windows and fans you get really great natural ventilation." As for the photovoltaic panels, Kipnis put them on the roof of a detached garage. A 6.2-kilowatt array, mounted at an optimal angle to the sun, produces enough electricity to power the 2,800-square-foot house and an electric car.

Energy modeling software helps Kipnis balance the complicated tradeoffs in sustainable design. He can change nearly any component on the computer—including the location and solar coefficient of windows—and view its impact on energy consumption and cost. The program is useful for determining the least-expensive energy upgrades.

The program spits out a HERS (Home energy rating system) number, the leading energy rating system for new homes. A new home built to meet most local building codes typically earns a HERS rating of 100; most green new homes do much better. A HERS rating of zero means that the home produces all the energy it needs to operate. Uncommon Ground achieved a HERS rating of 30. It could have been even lower had the clients not insisted on natural gas to cook and heat hot water. "I could have taken the house to net-zero but the couple decided not to put panels on the roof of the main house," says Kipnis. "We discussed having no natural gas. But they are cooks. I said, even the top chefs are using induction cooktops. Do you really need gas to char peppers? But they weren't going to budge."

The key to a super-low HERS rating is a super-airtight building. But with minimal air entering and leaving the building naturally, interior air quality is a concern. Most green homes contain an air exchanger that brings fresh air into the house,

capturing heat from outgoing air and transferring it to incoming air. The Uncommon Ground home was finished with paints, stains, and cabinets that off-gas a minimal amount of volatile organic compounds (VOCs). Its fireplaces rely on outside air for combustion. A rain screen on the outside wall prevents moisture from penetrating the building envelope where, once trapped, it can cause mold to form.

Only after a home is designed to consume as little energy as possible does it make sense to size the mechanical systems and select appliances and products. The Uncommon Ground home relies on a smaller HVAC system than commonly found in a home this size. Energy Star appliances and LED lighting reduced electrical needs. By stacking wet rooms, the architect could reduce the length of hot water pipes, reducing the opportunity for heat to escape. Water consumption was controlled with WaterSense plumbing fixtures, permeable pavers that percolate rainwater into the ground, and low-water landscaping.

An important part of any green home is having enough homeowner controls to actually live up to theoretical HERS scores. The Uncommon Ground house has a high-efficiency, forced-air HVAC system with multiple zones—if the living room is too hot, its temperature can be adjusted without affecting bedrooms that might be plenty cool. The thermostat can be controlled through an app from a smartphone on the couch or a car headed to the airport. A program for the solar inverter allows the owners to see how much power their home produces and the resulting carbon reduction.

No ultra-sustainable home is worth its salt without reclaimed or recycled materials. It's amazing how much great material can be obtained today that's otherwise destined for the landfill. The cabinet panels in the Uncommon Ground home were cut from American elm damaged by Dutch elm disease. Built-in cabinetry in the family room was made with white oak available after a heavy storm downed trees in West Chicago. Den walls were cloaked with barn wood rescued from a dilapidated dairy in Southwest Wisconsin.

If building a sustainable home seems like a noble task, there's some urgency to the quest. California required that all new homes be net-zero by 2020, a precedent likely to be followed by other states. The movement has received a huge shot in the arm from steadily falling photovoltaic costs, brought on by a rush of imports, improved solar-to-electric conversion, and bigger economies of manufacturing scale. Looked at over a ten-year period, photovoltaic panels may be cheaper than utility power for those willing to make an upfront investment, which of course is mitigated by federal, state, and local tax incentives.

If you think you are located in a part of the country where solar won't work due to clouds or industrial pollution, think again. One of the toughest places to pencil out solar is Seattle, where storm clouds cover rooftops for much of the year. (You can look online to determine exactly how many solar days your home is likely to receive.) But Germany has roughly the same "solar insolation" levels as Seattle, and it was the world leader in PV (photovoltaic) power until the mid 2010s, when it was passed by China. In any event, the United States has huge untapped potential.

The other good news is that as solar adoption increases, systems improve. Old-fashioned photovoltaic panels produce direct-current (DC) power that must be converted to alternating current (AC) with a stand-alone inverter. Newer panels may come with built-in inverters that make installation much quicker and cheaper; it may not have to be done by an electrician. Software now tracks solar production and energy consumption. You can come home in the evening, find out

Design of the super-green Deep Eddy
House by Barley|Pfeiffer Architec-
ture started with a study of how the
sun would impact heating, cooling,
and electrical needs. *Photo by
Ryann Ford*

how much electricity your home produced during the day, and adjust your nighttime use accordingly. Maybe you don't wash your clothes until the sun comes out. Real-time data in some systems provides a gentle reminder to close doors and windows so that conditioned air doesn't escape.

The missing piece of the solar equation—at least for people who want to be free of the utility grid—has been a reliable battery for storing electricity. Without a battery, green homes must rely on utility power on a cloudy day. Inefficient lead-acid batteries were once the only battery choice. A new generation of deep charging, lithium-ion batteries hold four times the electricity and last three times longer. Falling prices for solar panels may leave room in the budget for a battery that frees a home from the utility grid. For hardcore solar advocates, the future is now.

THE OPTIMAL APPROACH TO SUSTAINABILITY VARIES DRAMATICALLY BY GEOGRAPHY, climate, and budget. Austin architect Peter Pfeiffer of Barley|Pfeiffer Architecture likes to compare the needs of buildings to the needs of humans—they both need to be kept warm, or cool, depending on the outside temperature. That calls for a different approach in mild Austin compared to chilly Chicago. A net-positive house in the Windy City would need a super-thick coat of insulation in the winter. A home in Austin would need as much shade as possible to protect it from hot summer sun.

Pfeiffer recently consulted with clients from Chicago who wanted to build a house in Austin. They expressed a desire for a steeply pitched roof that reminded them of home. "That may make sense in Chicago, where you get big snow loads," he says. "But in Austin it's more important to get a big overhang to keep the sun out of the house during the summer. You can pay for that by economizing on the roof."

Pfeiffer uses window awnings, roof overhangs, and weather-resistant siding to reduce the need for air conditioning and electricity. "Shading the south-facing windows on my house saved more money than the solar panels on the roof will ever produce," says the architect, who often gives talks on green building techniques.

Interior designers, at their annual meetings, talk about the need to reduce glare for an aging population by specifying dark finishes. But dark colors also prevent the spread of usable sunlight within the home. Pfeiffer prefers to control glare through awnings, then work with a bright interior color palette that doesn't require as much electrical lighting. "Low-e glass and LED lighting are expensive ways to deal with the symptoms of bad daylighting," he says. Better use of natural lighting also results in more even temperatures from one room to the next. That means you won't have to adjust indoor temperatures to make one space hotter or cooler, wasting energy in the process.

Once you've reduced the energy demands of your home, the next step is to downsize mechanical and electrical systems. By harnessing solar radiation, you may be able to buy a smaller furnace. And by providing more shade, you may be able to get by with a smaller air conditioning system. Only after designing the most energy-efficient building possible does it make sense to buy expensive high-efficiency appliances, air conditioners, and furnaces. They require maintenance and their efficiency can decline over time.

Pfeiffer counsels clients to think twice about tankless water heaters, another darling of the green building movement. The Department of Energy strongly promotes their use, since they heat hot water only when needed. They may make abundant sense for power users of hot water—families with teenage athletes predisposed to taking therapeutic showers. But they may not be the best solution for empty-nester couples that don't shower as often, as they may need to be replaced before paying for themselves through utility savings.

Healthy indoor air is another goal of sustainable home design. The number one source of air pollution is an attached garage, especially if the house has central air. A logical first step for someone really concerned about indoor air quality is to detach the garage or create an air barrier between it and the house. Pfeiffer also specifies a physical insect barrier along the house foundation to reduce reliance on pesticides. And he lets new carpet and furniture air out in the garage for two days before they are brought into the home.

Green choices sometimes require lifestyle changes. Pfeiffer recalls a difficult conversation with an aging baby boomer couple who wanted a sustainable addition to their single-story house. He convinced them to build up rather than out, even though they were concerned about regularly climbing the stairs. Compared to a ranch, a two-story home has a smaller foundation and roof, reducing the opportunity for thermal transfer. "A two-story house costs less to operate, and less to build too," he says. "You have less air leakage around the foundation. And it's easier to vertically zone—you can just heat or cool the bedroom floor when you are using it at night."

In another case, he convinced clients accustomed to living in a 5,000-square-foot suburban abode to remodel a home close to town less than half that size. Its location in Deep Eddy, an eclectic, transitional Texas neighborhood, meant that they could walk to restaurants and a popular hiking and biking trail. They wouldn't need their cars as much. "They bought into the idea of reducing their carbon footprint with a high-performance home with healthy indoor air," Pfeiffer says. "The whole idea was to promote a more active lifestyle."

That includes climbing stairs to second-floor bedrooms, where windows can remain open at night without compromising home security. A screened-in porch on the southeast takes advantage of prevailing breezes, and a stair tower with shaded clerestory windows on the northwest draws air through the house. The most pleasant porches, Pfeiffer notes, often face prevailing breezes, providing the added benefit of keeping insects away. Porches require different treatments depending on the direction they face. A porch facing south, where it's safe from winter winds, needs protection from harsh summer sun. A west-facing porch, an ideal spot for watching the sun set, may get so hot in the summer that it won't be used.

Oversized awnings or overhangs protect virtually every window or door in the house from harsh Texas sunlight. Most windows face south or north to avoid any excessive early morning or late afternoon sunlight. That reduces the temptation to close the blinds then turn on an electric light to read or cook. Surfaces next to windows reflect light into interiors, reducing electric lighting needs. Pfeiffer located light fixtures, most of them holding LED bulbs, close to the task they are lighting. That reduces the intensity of required light.

Pfeiffer detached the garage so that pollutants—car exhaust, pesticides, and fertilizers—wouldn't get drawn into the main house. The open-air garage also serves as a patio, outdoor cooking area, and pet-washing station. Then he made sure the home was positively pressurized, without going overboard. Larger-than-necessary kitchen fans, for instance, can create negative air pressure that draws outside air pollutants. "Fans at 200 to 300 CFM [cubic feet per minute] are fine for the kitchen, even when you cook a lot," he says.

Controlling relative humidity is another secret to managing indoor air quality. A steady forty to sixty percent humidity— many smart thermostats now provide this reading—helps prevent mold from forming and dust mites from breeding. The single biggest source of home humidity is the washing machine. Front-loading washers may produce less moist air than top loading varieties. Long, hot showers are another big source of humidity. A $150 upgrade buys bathroom fans that automatically cycle on when humidity levels get too high. Motion detectors can keep fans on for five minutes after you finish a shower to clear the room of moisture. Whole-house dehumidifiers, a common approach in the past, are passé. "Today we are getting rid of the humidity at its source with kitchen and bath fans," Pfeiffer says.

Awnings, high windows, and ceiling fans cool key spaces, reducing air-conditioning needs. *Photo by Ryann Ford*

When moisture builds up in a house, the air conditioning system must work harder to dry the air. If you can reduce humidity, you may be able to downsize HVAC equipment and save money. Leaky air ducts are another big drag on air conditioning. "Twenty percent duct leakage compromises air conditioning by forty percent," says Pfeiffer, who centralizes HVAC equipment to shorten duct runs and reduce the opportunity for leaks. "Leak-free ductwork is more important than the efficiency of your HVAC equipment."

Pfeiffer doesn't leave the design of the roof to chance, either. Many builders of energy efficient homes install a synthetic membrane under the roof and apply spray foam to the attic ceiling. But that traps moisture. "You need to ventilate the roof," says the architect, who included both a sealed attic and a ventilated roof on the Deep Eddy House. "It acts like an umbrella, keeping unwanted solar radiation from entering the house."

Water is another natural resource that should be controlled at the source, says Pfeiffer. Low-flow faucets and fixtures in the Deep Eddy home, along with a water-saving clothes washer, reduce water needs. A gutter/downspout system collects rainwater to irrigate native, drought-tolerant plants in the yard. "But the primary goal was to reduce water consumption in the first place," he says.

Advanced framing techniques—lining up load-bearing elements from one floor to the next, and taking unnecessary lumber out of corners and around doors and windows—resulted in fifteen to twenty percent less lumber. The green agenda also included recycling construction waste—cardboard, metal, gypsum, and scrap lumber. The builder stockpiled soil during excavation for later use and turned scrap lumber and drywall into mulch for use as backfill. Virtually all material used to build the home came from within 500 miles of the jobsite, reducing fuel needed to get it there.

GREEN-HOME STANDARDS OFTEN SERVE AS USEFUL GUIDES TO SUSTAINABILITY DECISIONS. That was the case with another of Kipnis' projects, the Glencoe House, one of the first LEED Platinum homes in suburban Chicago. The LEED program includes a checklist of potential green features that add up to produce a rating, with Platinum being the highest. The Glencoe House received points for its defining feature—a green roof, rare for a detached suburban home. Though hidden from the street, the green roof is visible from the master bedroom and main hallway, thanks the second floor's U-shaped design.

Kipnis positioned the solar panels to optimize their performance. He reserved the steeper south-facing surface for solar hot water panels. The angle is optimal for low winter sun, the time of year when hot water would be most valuable. During the summer, on the other hand, electricity from photovoltaic panels would come in handy to run air conditioning. Kipnis put those panels on the shallower south-facing roof section. They are more parallel to the high summer sun, to maximize their production in the middle of the day.

The home's solar orientation once again guided Kipnis' approach to design. Overhangs shade the home during hot summer months based on the summer solstice angle. "They significantly reduce the heat gain on the house, making it easier to do natural ventilation and reducing the amount of air conditioning required," says Kipnis. When air conditioning is needed, a tight frame sprayed with closed-cell insulation prevents cool air from escaping. Closed-cell foam achieves very high R-values—forty in the walls, fifty-five in the roof.

The house relies on thermal mass—one-and-a-half-inch concrete floors—for heat. The concrete absorbs sunlight on cold winter days and releases it slowly at night. The concrete floors also contain radiant heat tubes that are warm to the feet on winter mornings. Hot air rises naturally to the upper floors, where windows are positioned to accept more passive

A rainwater-collecting green roof, accessible from the master bedroom, doubles as a second-floor terrace. *Photo courtesy Kipnis Architecture + Planning*

Vegetation cools the porch during summer months. *Photo courtesy Kipnis Architecture + Planning*

PLANS / The roof design optimizes the angle of solar panels and hot-water collectors for months when they are needed most. *Diagram courtesy Kipnis Architecture + Planning*

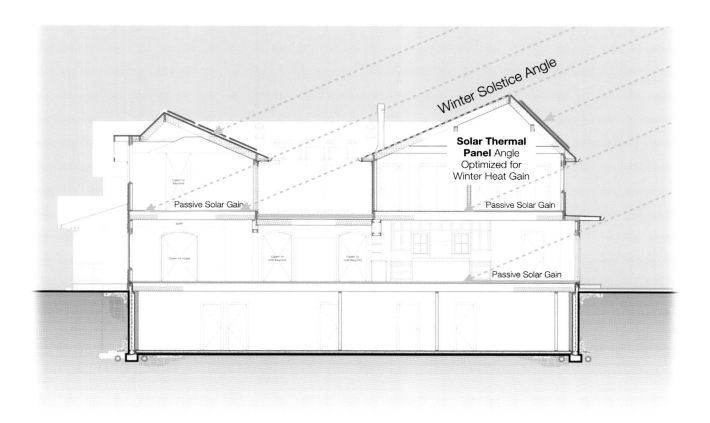

Winter Solstice Angle

Solar Thermal Panel Angle Optimized for Winter Heat Gain

Passive Solar Gain

Passive Solar Gain

Passive Solar Gain

solar heat. On hotter days, cool air enters through basement windows on the north side and circulates naturally through transoms over the doors, exiting through operable clerestory windows at the top of the stairs.

The Glencoe House conserves water as well as electricity. A rain barrel collects water that's used for native and low-maintenance landscaping, and rainwater from a metal roof irrigates the green roof. Permeable driveway and yard pavers minimize site run off. Super-efficient faucets, toilets, dishwashers, and clothes washers conserve water. The home doesn't recycle wastewater, as some of the most water-efficient homes do. County restrictions made that a tough goal to achieve. Some super-green homes capture water from showers and sometimes sinks, clean it, and reuse it for toilets and irrigation.

With its gabled roof, welcoming front porch, and metal roof, the Glencoe House strikes a very traditional pose, one that belies its state-of-the-art sustainable design. It looks right at home in this Chicago neighborhood of traditional homes, even as it points to a future when most new homes produce most, if not all the energy they need.

10.
PULL FROM
VERNACULAR STYLES

A metal roof, local limestone, and
dark eaves connect the Olmos Park
Home by Lake|Flato Architects with
hill country architectural tradition.
Photo by Casey Dunn

Expansive glass windows and doors,
tall ceilings, and white interiors focus
attention on the exterior view. A chef's
kitchen with a walk-in refrigerator
looks directly out to the two
courtyards. *Photo by Casey Dunn*

THE MOST IMPRESSIVE HOMES CELEBRATE REGIONAL ARCHITECTURE AND MATERIALS

ONE OF THE MOST REFRESHING TRENDS OF THE LAST TWO DECADES IS THE RISING POPULARITY OF VERNACULAR DESIGN. The best of these homes look like they really belong where they were built, maybe even like they've been there forever, often because they were built with native materials. Many rely on building forms and treatments originally developed in response to local climate conditions—cool side porches that capture precious breezes, elevated foundations that stand above the water line, shingled siding that resists sea air, or adobe walls that store solar heat for cool desert nights.

The coastal cottage, also known as the Florida cracker house, is a personal favorite. Raised slightly above ground to prevent flooding, with a metal roof to shed rain, its defining characteristic was a long front porch to enjoy summer evenings. A long hallway running from front to back often provided the only air conditioning. It's a close cousin to the narrow, shotgun-style homes that pervade Louisiana. In New England you find saltbox homes with a one-story lean-to on the back to accommodate growing families. The region is also known for its sturdy seaside cottages.

An expansive network of bedroom blinds provides relief from the hot Texas sun. *Photo by Casey Dunn*

The house works with the lot's contours, which created the opportunity for an elevated porch deck. *Photo by Casey Dunn*

Landscaping creates the impression this home sits on a secluded lot rather than a suburban street. *Photo by Casey Dunn*

When architects take these vernacular forms to a higher level, it's as though a classical composer elevated a folk song to a symphony. One of the most celebrated indigenous styles is the hill country home of Central Texas, defined by white limestone, dark wood trim, and a metal roof. Many started as weekend homes built by European immigrants on small ranches and rural property, often by masons and carpenters who gathered white limestone and cedar nearby. Now you find grand interpretations in some of the most prestigious Texas neighborhoods. The style lends itself to contemporary design because of its simple material palette, use of contrasting colors, and preference for leaving structural elements exposed. One challenge with doing an authentic interpretation is that the design wants to respond to natural surroundings that may not be present in the suburbs.

That was the case when a client came to Lake|Flato architects looking to do hill country architecture on a three-quarter-acre corner lot in suburban San Antonio. There are no long views of hills or prairies here—only the community's prosaic storm water collection reservoir. Thankfully, the Olmos Park Residence's slightly contoured lot was covered with trees—heritage oaks, elms, and fruit trees—that many builders would have removed to speed construction and design a bigger, fancier house. Lake|Flato decided instead to systematically use the trees to create shade, privacy, views, and a rural sensibility. The T-shaped house capitalizes on the lot's only open view—through the reservoir to the woods beyond. The result gives the impression of living in the woods on a large plot of land.

Hill country homes were built with stone on the first-story walls for security, then went to timber on the upper level. Lake|Flato used glass transoms above stone lower walls to convey the same effect. The glass not only lights private rooms but makes the roof appear to float. The home's deep eaves serve a purpose: they strategically cover a backyard path. Windows and fireplaces, set deep into the limestone exterior, accentuate the home's sturdy stone mass.

The design evinces the style's preference for exposed structural components. The building's steel frame, exposed inside and out, seamlessly merges with metal window frames. Limestone finds its way inside the house to form a fireplace wall and a staircase. A large slice of wood, protected with polyurethane, suffices for a kitchen countertop. The interiors, like the exteriors, benefit from the pleasing contrast of dark wood tones and creamy stone colors.

The Olmos Park Residence does it best to take advantage of the natural elements. Cool air enters through operable low windows, circulates through an open floor plan, and exits through windows in the home's upper reaches. An extensive network of blinds controls solar gain in key spots. Rain chains, in lieu of downspouts, collect water in barrels.

Extensive glass doors and windows provide courtyard views from public rooms. The floor plan tucks two long, narrow rooms of masonry and steel between the largest heritage oaks. Stone arches connect many rooms, preserving lines of sight to the outdoors. Concrete vaults, crafted from recycled oil drums, form the ceiling of several rooms. Modern accoutrements include a detached workout facility and a separate guest suite.

Cedar siding, vinyl trim, and galvanized steel means the family won't be spending weekends maintaining the Marsh House. *Photo by Warren Jagger*

Changes in ceiling heights and treatments—such as the white beam between the kitchen and living room—express activity zones within the great room plan. *Photo by Warren Jagger*

Window seats, porches, and decks make the most of water views. *Photo by Warren Jagger*

THE WORK OF THE RHODE ISLAND-BASED FIRM ESTES TWOMBLY ISN'T EASILY CATEGORIZED. The Marsh House, which sits on a magnificent fifteen-acre site next to a wetland near Crane Beach, is a prime example. Pale cedar siding, painted white trim, and a standing seam metal roof have their roots in traditional New England seaside architecture. But the sparseness of details outside and inside evinces a quiet modernism. It's as though the architects have boiled down a vernacular form to its bare, essential ingredients.

Only because lightning destroyed the home that previously occupied the property could a new one be built this close to protected marsh. The owners managed to work a deal with the conservation commission to expand the new home's footprint. They agreed to pull a boathouse out of the marsh (it was repurposed as a shed) and remove one of the two driveways, restoring the land to its original wetlands state. In return, the commission allowed the owners to build a guest wing to the main house on the island side, away from the marsh.

Now a lone driveway cuts through the property, ending in a courtyard defined by unmistakably Yankee forms—a gabled main house and a shed-like guest wing. A glass entry joins the buildings, framing a distant view of Choate Island. To enhance this view, Estes realigned the entry with a "duckwalk"—an elevated path that crosses tidal rivers running through the marshes. It leads to a dock where the family parks its skiff and the kids jump in the water. The guest wing, clad in corrugated steel, the same material used on the roof of the main house, isn't just for guests; it includes a photography studio.

The interiors of the main house depart from the regimented floor plans of traditional New England cottages. An open plan with high exposed ceilings does a better job of tying internal spaces to exterior views, creating the impression that the home is much bigger than 3,000 square feet. "We try to avoid designing a house of rooms, a series of small spaces. We want to open up the main living spaces and make them three-dimensional," Estes says.

West- and south-facing windows provide precious solar exposure during winter months. Radiant heaters below composite maple floors furnish back-up heat during the coldest months. The home's narrow profile—only a room wide in many places—promotes cross ventilation during summer months. But when the weather is nice, the family spends most of its time on the expansive deck that wraps the main house.

Changes in ceiling texture, instead of walls, demarcate cooking, living, and dining spaces. A sliding barn door—a reference to the home's rural heritage—is all that separates an office from the main living area. Estes also takes inspiration from the taut, functional design of boats. Poles in the master bedroom ceiling create a nautical impression, and a long window seat is an ideal perch from which to view the marsh and passing ships.

With deep eaves, big overhangs, and windows organized into groups of three, the Graber House gives foursquare homes a prairie-style update. *Photo courtesy Woodley Architectural Group*

A long, cantilevered roof protects a huge rear deck accessed through perpendicular window walls in the great room. *Photo courtesy Woodley Architectural Group*

Tall great room ceilings drop in the kitchen to bring lighting closer to work surfaces. *Photo courtesy Woodley Architectural Group*

IN DENVER, THE AMERICAN FOURSQUARE IS SO COMMON THAT THE STYLE IS OFTEN REFERRED TO AS THE DENVER SQUARE. Many of these space-efficient homes, two and a half stories with a large central dormer, were built after the silver crash of 1893 as economical and practical alternatives to the Victorian homes that preceded them. Designed to get the most living space out of a narrow lot, the homes feature interiors divided into quadrants with four rooms per floor. The design was popular in streetcar suburbs within five miles of downtown. Today they are some of the choicest neighborhoods in the city.

A client with a lot in one of these neighborhoods asked architect Mike Woodley for a home that would blend with the streetscape but take the foursquare in a modern direction. It was a time-honored request; architects have been improving on the basic foursquare design for more than a century. In one of the most famous cases, Frank Lloyd Wright, in a project for *Ladies' Home Journal*, redrew it to create more cubic forms. He flattened the roof, brought order to the windows, married the home to the ground, and opened up the closed-off interiors. The result was considered an important precursor to his prairie style of architecture.

For the Graber house, Woodley picked up on the neighborhood's material palette of brick, stucco, and cedar. The home isn't much bigger than the foursquare homes that surround it, but its massing is different. A wing with windows on three sides juts into the front yard. A bay window in the middle of the front façade breaks down the quadrants. A shift from brick to cedar siding on the second floor gives the home a horizontal orientation. And a large cantilevered roof, reminiscent of Wright's work, defines the back porch. "The design is modern," says Woodley, "but it doesn't turn off people looking for transitional architecture."

11.
BUILD ON
EXISTING DNA

The remodel of a small post-modern
home, House on Poplar Avenue by
Mark McInturff, builds on the original
boxy form. *Photo by Julia Heine*

SUCCESSFUL REMODELING PROJECTS BUILD ON THE BEST OF WHAT'S ALREADY THERE

A ton of remodeling work gets done each year, most of it sight unseen. Families enclose a porch to become a year-round playroom for young children. Couples borrow space from a hallway closet to create a master bathroom that's a more comfortable place to get ready for work each morning. Unfinished basements finally receive the drywall, flooring, and lighting they need to take on band practice, billiards, or a home business. Worn-out windows, siding, and roofing get replaced to give a home a new lease on life. Few of these projects ever grace the pages of national magazines; much less win a national design award. But they significantly improve the quality of life that families lead.

The kind of remodeling project that does win a national award remains true to the original structure, when it's worth preserving. Additions seem like a natural evolution, with materials and building forms that fuse with the original structure. They must build on the original design, whether it's Gothic revival or mid-century modern, otherwise the finished result looks ungainly or confused. In design competitions, it's not uncommon for judges looking at before-and-after pictures to decide they like the before pictures better.

Architect Stephen Muse refers to his work remodeling homes as "corrective surgery." Triage starts with determining what's worth preserving. What elements contribute to the home's architectural charm? At the same time, what needs to be improved, visually and functionally? The reality is that not everything designed for a home fifty years ago should be kept. "When you remodel homes—especially historic homes—some firms want to match the existing home exactly," Muse says. "But it doesn't make sense to copy the problems in old homes. Do you really want small windows in a home with tremendous views? Do you really want a bunch of small, rarely used rooms when you have a chance to start over? I think not."

Muse took an educated scalpel to the Westmoreland House, a center-hall colonial on a dead-end street in the Maryland suburbs of Washington, DC. The house failed to take advantage of its proximity to a wooded park. The only focal point from the large entry foyer was an old staircase. Many spaces in the cramped home suffered from lack of natural light. Most rooms stood alone; they didn't relate to each other. The kitchen and family rooms begged to be brought up to today's living standards.

Although the floor plan needed major surgery, Muse determined that the exterior skeleton of the 1930s home was worth preserving. "There's a hip on the front. It's nice. Why change it?" he says. He liked the color and pattern of the original brickwork as well, though sourcing more of it—as he asked the contractor to do—was easier said than done. Muse decided to stick with the geometric patterns and colors in the original windows but ganged them on the addition to create bigger and better views. As a result, the addition looks like it's always been there.

The original floor plan suffered from circulatory problems, the biggest one being that most rooms ignored the park. The new family room on the park side, with windows on three sides, feels enshrouded by the woods. It's reached by walking down a short flight of stairs, which makes the ceiling appear higher and adds to the cocoon-like sensation.

The owners—an editor, a journalist, and their two daughters—wanted a home that could handle large parties. Muse added larger windows to the living room, relocated the dining room to the end of the entry hall, and connected the rooms with large framed openings rather than doors. The reconfigured rooms borrow light and space from each other, creating better party circulation.

Moving the stairs from the entry hall to the back of the home added usable space on the first floor. It also allowed the architect to create a view through the interior, painted white with minimal trim so that it doesn't interfere with the sight lines. The new staircase—with open risers, a glass-block wall, and numerous skylights—serves as a light well, reducing the need for electric lighting. A geothermal HVAC system, foam insulation, and new low-e windows round out the energy program. The remodel reclaims hardwood flooring and porch timber from the original structure.

ONE OF THE MOST EXTREME EXAMPLES OF SENSITIVE REMODELING may be the work done to restore Washington, DC, architect Hugh Newell Jacobsen's masterpiece, Four Pavilions. Named a Record House in 1978 by *Architectural Record* for reasons still evident today, the former Drier Home sits on the edge of a wooded lot overlooking the Potomac River in Virginia. When Jacobsen designed the 1,990-square-foot home in 1975, it was about the size of the typical new home in the United States. He wanted to show the world just how much architecture you could get at that modest size.

Jacobsen tied together a series of white gabled sheds with a trapezoidal porch. He relied on uniform external surfaces and minimal ornamentation to emphasize the pleasing geometry of the forms. The little boxes meet to create dynamic, witty interior spaces. A soaring monolith in the foyer leads to a vaulted living space with big triangular windows. Skylights and bay windows cast unexpected shadows throughout the house. Small, inspired details contribute to the home's charm. Air grills borrow a vertical slat pattern from closet doors. The same striation became the inspiration for the master bedroom headboard.

Soaring interior volumes, triangular windows, and patio doors preserve Jacobsen's witty intent. *Photo courtesy of Richard Williams Architects*

The bedroom wall picks up on the striation pattern used on vent covers and the chimney. *Photo courtesy of Richard Williams Architects*

Updated kitchens and baths remain true to the original design. *Photo courtesy of Richard Williams Architects*

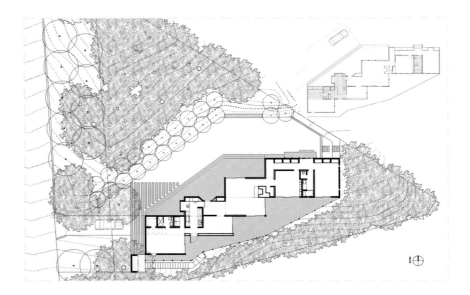

By 2010, the house was falling apart. Severe structural problems, many caused by water leaks in an interior gutter system, created a very real threat it would be razed, especially since it occupied a prized river-view lot. The home sat on the market for several years as would-be buyers, often accompanied by architects, estimated the restoration costs. Architect Richard Williams walked the project with clients who waited on the sidelines for the price to drop to the point where they could afford the remodel. When it finally did, they pounced.

Extensive water damage called for a stem-to-stern renovation. That included replacing most of the home's wood frame and applying new insulation. The exterior skin, though virtually identical to what was there before, was replaced with a rain screen that encourages moisture to exit the building envelope. The home received new insulated windows and doors, a new roof, new flashing, and built-in gutters. The decks were reframed and reclad. Inside, nearly all the finishes were replaced. New electrical lines, plumbing, and appliances were installed.

Williams tweaked the interiors to bring them up to today's living standards, as is done in most preservation projects. He created new layouts for the kitchen, laundry, and guest bath. The kitchens and baths were remodeled with new fixtures and appliances. A cast concrete retaining wall was added to raise the sloped grade at the master bedroom end of the house. A new sliding door and a small deck provide access to the newly elevated lawn. "The most visible change was to better integrate the house to the landscape," Williams says. "We replaced one of two oriel windows in the master with a new glass door with a sliding shutter. You can walk gracefully from the master suite to a new garden terrace."

Jacobson had wisely pushed the building to the edge of the lot to preserve the best part of the site for vegetation and views. The remodel kept the home in its original position, but Williams worked closely with Charlottesville, Virginia, landscape architect Gregg Bleam to better integrate the home and yard. The original driveway, a simple gravel pad, only provided access to the street. But the new driveway leads to a series of pavers that cross the lawn with a geometry that mimics the gable form. "The house was substantially rebuilt," says Williams. "But the intent of the details, the form of the massing, and the genius of the plan were honored."

AS APPRECIATION OF MODERN ARCHITECTURE DEEPENS, so does the desire to preserve its early history. The late California architect Barry Berkus, widely considered the father of production (subdivision) housing architecture, was an early pioneer of modern design. Late in his life, he was driving past Park Imperial South, a condominium resort community that he designed in Palm Springs at age twenty-five, fresh out of architecture school. The edgy project had won an award for technological innovation when it was built in 1960, but he hadn't been back to see it in almost fifty years. "The project was pretty wild for its time," he remembered. Folded plywood roofs appeared to float above clerestory windows, creating unusual interior volumes and deep exterior roof overhangs. Post and beam construction supported large fixed glass walls and doors that connected to private courtyards behind each home.

"I knocked on the door of one of the homes, and this professor inside was going through a full renovation, polishing hinges and trying to figure out how it all worked," Berkus said. "I sat down and we talked about it. He said several owners were doing the renovations themselves, with the help of architects who lived there. They were bringing it all back to life—the terrazzo floors, the 1957 brass hinges, the mahogany cabinets. One architect even found an original GE range that had been sitting in the garage for thirty years. It was the original turquoise with the [color-coordinated] range hood that I had designed."

As he toured homes, Berkus realized he'd sown the seeds for concepts he would pursue later in his career, especially the notion that homes shouldn't be containers "but rather backdrops for particular tastes and lifestyles." At Park Imperial

Walled rear courtyards provide private outdoor space at Park Imperial South, a post-modern condominium community built in 1960. *Photo by Barry Berkus*

Sliding shoji screens separate the living room from a flex room that, Berkus later discovered, lived up to its name. *Photo by Barry Berkus*

Concrete block half-walls divide the family rooms from kitchens. Berkus designed the quirky range hoods. *Photo by Barry Berkus*

South, he had designed flexible homes, less than 1,500 square feet with a couple of bedrooms and baths, that had successfully accommodated the lifestyles of architects, professors, musicians, singles, empty nesters, and young families. The homes included dens—separated from the main living area by sliding shoji screens—that homeowners had used for offices, guest rooms, yoga studios, and libraries. Other flights of fancy had stood the test of time, such as the half-walls that formed entry vestibules and the concrete block used to build kitchen islands and cocktail bars.

The community was pretty dense for its time—thirty homes on three-and-a-half acres with a shared pool in the middle. Each home had a private back patio, and several had carports. Two homes had laundry rooms at one end. The homes were sited to maximize privacy with windows on at least two sides. When homes faced public spaces, Berkus designed them with tall walls of concrete block topped by clerestory windows. He found that many homeowners had turned their private courtyards into oases with desert plants and water features.

Most homes shared a wall, often with a privacy fin that extended into the yard. Early on, homeowners had enclosed outdoor dining rooms with concrete block, converting them into interior space. Later most wood patio walls in the rear had been replaced with concrete block. Each home had a colorful front door that stood out against a backdrop of concrete block. Meandering cement walkways led past gravel front yards to the community pool house and spa that had been enclosed for safety. Residents felt so strongly about preserving Park Imperial South that they led a charge to preserve it as a historic district. The city granted their wish.

Obie Bowman's remodel of the Sonoma Coast House preserved the original prized redwood siding but took better advantage of a prime location on a bluff overlooking a small cove. *Photo courtesy Obie G. Bowman Architect*

A new tower directs light into a dining room with views to an old Monterey pine and coastal hills. *Photo courtesy Obie G. Bowman Architect*

When the rolling barn door is closed, its spokes fill cubbyholes along the wall. *Photo courtesy Obie G. Bowman Architect*

THE DECISION WHETHER TO PRESERVE A HOME OR TEAR IT DOWN AND START ANEW IS RARELY AN EASY ONE.
California architect Obie Bowman was working late one night when he got a call—a potential client wanted him to come right over and look at the vacation house he had bought. He needed an expert's advice about whether to tear it down or remodel it again. Bowman arrived to find that the vacation house, built in 1971 on a bluff overlooking the Sonoma coast, had structural problems. One wall was sloping, its cheap windows hardly worth salvaging. The home had a hodgepodge of level changes, poorly organized with dark, awkward rooms. But Bowman figured that if the house were torn down, a cool $100,000 in materials would wind up in the landfill. He convinced the owner to remodel instead.

The original redwood walls were braced and extended. But many interior walls were removed in favor of an open floor plan that emphasizes views of the surrounding light and trees. From a new entry, situated between a kitchen and dining room, visitors descend into a split-function living room, with a fireplace and television to the right, and a new glazed octagonal conversation area to the left, framed with timber girts and Douglas fir columns. Big windows

in the conversation area, visible from the kitchen and dining area, usher sunlight deep into the house. The owners also got a new basement recreation level.

The remodel, which only added 850 square feet to the original home's footprint, addressed the old home's chief failing. "The original home treated its lot as little more than a placemat," says the architect. Visitors now approach from the east along a meandering stone path that passes beneath the boughs of a magnificent old Monterey pine. They eventually arrive at a massive redwood and concrete trellis designed to support giant honeysuckles. Bowman wanted to add roof overhangs to limit solar gain, but a local design committee said no. Instead, he designed a natural ventilation system to limit heat gain from the extensively glazed southwest side. It was important because the house often goes unoccupied for weeks at a time until its owners find time to vacation.

MANY HOMEOWNERS DECIDE TO BUY AN EXISTING HOME AND REMODEL IT BECAUSE THE HOME SITS ON A SPECIAL LOT. That was the case with builder Alan Kanner, who was attracted to a small, nondescript home that sat deep in the woods of Takoma Park, Maryland, a close-in suburb of Washington, DC. When the home went on the market, he bought it and hired his friend Mark McInturff to design a remodel. The pair found that the old post-modern home suffered from a tired layout, with the main living areas cramped on a lower walkout level and three small bedrooms on the second floor. Kanner wanted more livable floor space, room for an occasional house concert, and space for his children to do homework. He also wanted a "more playful" house. McInturff was more than happy to comply.

The remodeled home, with beams that extend through the exterior wall, now makes the most of its natural setting. *Photo courtesy Obie G. Bowman Architect*

At House on Poplar Avenue by Mark McInturff, open V-shaped cradles support the deck, making it easy for light to enter the refurbished basement. *Photo by Julia Heine*

McInturff's remodel of House on Poplar Avenue keeps the home's boxy shape, a trademark of post-modern design. He added a third floor, working within the footprint of the existing house, and moved the bedrooms up there, giving some vaulted clerestory windows. The move freed space on the second floor for an open plan with living, dining, and kitchen spaces, and a semi-enclosed TV room. A bay window, projecting slightly from the wall, rises from the living room to the master bedroom. Picture windows and a long deck now marry living spaces to the surrounding woods. A reworked lower level with an open family room walks out to the sloping, wooded backyard.

The remodeled house makes a whimsical impression from the street; it resembles a big black cube with a colorful bay window, the color scheme inspired by one of Richard Diebenkorn's Ocean Park paintings. Other bright colors—a red canopy over the front door and a light blue accent under a window—dot the exterior. Close inspection reveals that the aluminum siding mixes horizontal and vertical laps, alternated to create texture. McInturff, who purposely used narrow laps because of the home's small scale, compares the look to corduroy.

A floating staircase with open risers, white oak treads, and a wire mesh wall anchors the second floor. *Photo by Julia Heine*

An open floor plan with modern touches—steel poles, floating cabinets—works for the occasional house concert. *Photo by Julia Heine*

A new entry, suspended in the woods, makes a colorful and tactile first impression. *Photo by Julia Heine*

The home is now approached from a narrow bridge—McInturff likens it to a gangplank—that leads to a cantilevered deck. Supported by V-shaped cradles, the deck appears suspended in the woods. While inexpensive wood posts could have been used to support the deck, the open cradles, built with steel pipes and I-beams, make it easier for light to penetrate the basement.

A floating staircase lit by a large window highlights the main living areas. Otherwise, bright blues, reds, and greens punctuate a neutral palette of white walls and light wood flooring. Other post-modern accents include a floating blue cabinet by the door and steel poles in the living room. The kitchen mixes black and light blue cabinetry with stainless steel appliances. A raised ceiling makes the kitchen look like it was cut into a cube. The end result: a post-modern box that's true to its original design intent but does a much better job of accommodating a modern lifestyle.

12.
BREAK THE
PRODUCTION MOLD

TODAY'S SUBDIVISION HOUSING OFFERS FLEXIBLE, LIVABLE FLOOR PLANS

It's easy to be cynical about model homes in builder communities—the jaguar throw rugs in the master bedroom, the trophy cases for fictitious child soccer stars in the hallway, the roosters and wire baskets in the French kitchen. Then you stumble upon something fresh—a staircase design you haven't seen before, a home office arrangement that makes eminent sense, or a big laundry room that would come in quite handy. You find out the home is within financial reach; buying it would give you access to a great lap pool at the community center, and you decide, "I could live here." It's a decision that hundreds of thousands of American households make each year. The reality is that production builders, rather than custom builders, provide most of the new homes available for purchase.

Simple massing, flat roofs, and restrained decoration give these California production homes a contemporary flair. *Photo courtesy of The New Home Company*

The hunt for the next big idea takes builders and architects to visit new-home communities throughout the country. I was walking a series of new homes in Southern California with some builders recently when the contingent stopped in its tracks. A granite bar occupied the back corner of a family room. Windows behind the bar folded back accordion style, creating a pass-through counter like you might see at a tropical hotel. As if to complete the resort experience, the pass-through led to a covered outdoor space replete with sofas, chaise lounges, a dining table, outdoor kitchen, and fire pit. The setting reminded me of a relaxing evening spent with friends by a fire on a mild winter night at the Arizona Biltmore Hotel in Phoenix. This wouldn't be a bad way to live.

That's the thing about production housing—builders, like fashion retailers, search out and promote the next cool thing, or, more accurately, the next cool thing that doesn't cost too much. They try to anticipate new lifestyle directions, highlight them in models, and hope people buy into the dream. When iPads first appeared, astute builders gave them away at closing to control home systems. Ten years ago, when baby boomers were drinking more wine than water, wine dispensers and coolers showed up in the kitchen. Later, it was drop zones by the back door with cubbies for shoes and backpacks, or a large shower enclosure in the master bath with enough nozzles to rival a car wash. Now the big thing is patio doors that fold open or roll into the wall to reveal an outdoor room.

It's difficult for production housing to win design awards, since it often competes against custom houses with bigger budgets. I used to keep a log of the digs judges uttered as they rejected projects. The rhetoric reached a high-water mark during the housing boom when builders were throwing money at design. Recessed ceilings in bedrooms got out of hand. You'd see three tiers of built-up cove molding, complete with flashing lights. "Is this your first visit to the star chamber?" one architect remarked as he threw out a South Florida luxury home. Another judge, looking at a man cave with the panache of a sports bar at the Holiday Inn, said, "This is one step above *Dogs Playing Poker*," a reference to the ubiquitous Coolidge painting.

During the housing boom of the 2000s, when every new home seemingly sold quickly, builders often dressed up the front elevation of homes to create curb appeal. They did little to articulate the other three sides, particularly the rear of the home, which the owners, of course, rarely see. Looking at a particularly weak rear elevation, one judge commented that it was "flatter than a baboon's ass!" Another year, during the judging of a West Coast design competition, the small production home entries were particularly weak. The host had invited the judges to throw submittals that didn't pass muster into a small trash can conveniently located in the front of the room. The jury was only mildly surprised when one judge attempted to throw a three-foot-high stack of folders—the entire small production home category—into the trash can. No award was given in the category that year, which led to an industry outcry. The rules were changed so that an award was given no matter what.

Production builders have three wild cards in the hole—price, land, and quick delivery—and bet on them continuously. They may offer move-in on a spec home within a month, knowing it would take an individual two or more years to find land, hire an architect, and build a custom home. They economize by building the same basic home at a regular tempo up and down the street, working with the same subcontractors who are familiar with the blueprints. When builders know in advance what they are building, they can secure volume discounts on materials and pass on some of the savings.

The problem is, a focus on first costs may result in homes that cost more to operate during the seven or more years that families live in them. Builders may leave off awnings or build short roof overhangs that could shade interior spaces and save on electric bills in the long run. They may nix photovoltaic panels even if that's a cheaper way to produce power over seven years than buying it from the utility. Buyers often share this myopic focus on first costs, shopping based on costs per square foot, when the real cost to live in the home is much more than a monthly mortgage payment. It includes utilities, property taxes, insurance, maintenance, and replacement costs for anything that breaks.

One consistent drawback of spec housing remains the lack of attention paid to how the house relates to the sun, its lot, and nature. Builders may build the same basic house up and down both sides of the street. Front elevations may face south on one side of the street, north on other, despite vastly different solar potential. National builders may disregard natural amenities around the home in their quest for economies of scale. One year I worked with a production builder to do a show home in Orlando on a lot backed by woods and a lake. The company wanted to produce a design that would work on any lot in the country. It took a lot of convincing before they would change the plan to include a window wall and a porch in the back to take advantage of lake views. Those turned out to be the home's best features.

Floor plans are often the strongest element of a production home. Builders may spend months trying to make every square foot more livable, stealing headroom from a stairway to create a bigger master closet, flipping rooms to provide better porch access. They often formulate optional room configurations for key spaces, showing would-be buyers how to turn an extra garage bay into a larger family room or convert an office into a first-floor master bedroom. Many tweak designs after early feedback from buyers and shoppers, like retailers who change inventory and store layout based on how customers shop.

PRODUCTION BUILDERS ENGAGE IN A RISKY BUSINESS, TO BE SURE. After dropping millions of dollars on land, they take an educated guess at what buyers at that location might want. It's a pretty existential situation. "We design to meet the expectations of buyers we haven't met, and often don't meet for a year or two," says Tom Redwitz, chief operating officer of The New Home Company based in Aliso Viejo, California. Focus group research reduces the company's risk. But Redwitz also knows, based on experience, to lavish attention on three key areas of the home—the kitchen, the master bedroom suite, and the outdoor room. "The kitchen may be the most important room, because it's become the center of family life," says Redwitz, who studied architecture. He makes sure the master bedroom suite is located in a private space. It needs to have strong emotional appeal, especially the bathroom and closets. And in the markets where the New Home Company works—primarily California and Arizona— great outdoor living space is essential. "If you get those three areas of the house right, you are on the way to a great home," he says. "In the best plans, you can almost triangulate them."

The New Home Company specializes in luxury production homes on breathtaking lots overlooking the Pacific Ocean. It's a rarefied price point for merchant builders, one that leads Redwitz to top architectural talent. He retained Bob White of Forest Studio to design Coral Crest, an enclave of twenty-eight homes starting at $4 million along the upper northeast point of Crystal Cove. White, whose work shows up in the pages of *Elle Decor*, combines a

The street entrance at Coral Crest leads to an entry courtyard intimately linked to interior spaces. *Photo courtesy of The New Home Company*

sophisticated matrix of courtyards, loggias, patios, and balconies with large, casually elegant public rooms and the latest creature comforts. Though he refrains from categorizing his designs, White says clients approach him with requests for "that California look."

The homes at Coral Crest require exploration. A false front door leads to an internal courtyard with fire pits and fountains, protected from strong winds that barrel up the hills from the ocean. Views from the courtyard extend through the heavily windowed house to the distant ocean. The many indoor-outdoor connections create a host of opportunities, and potential problems. In most cases, the outdoor spaces are easily accessed from major public rooms. Window walls fold back in the great room, dining room, and sometimes even the kitchen to join interior spaces with courtyards, porches, and loggias. White designs homes as linear forms—Ls, Ts, or Hs—that provide light and natural ventilation on two or three sides. That's what architects did in the days before air conditioning.

"At Coral Canyon, as you traverse the public spaces, there are no hallways," says White. "That gives you a feeling of openness and expansiveness. Then I'll change what I'm doing with the ceilings, with volume, or with wall details so that you feel differences in the spaces as you move through the house. That's subconsciously what people are talking about when they say they want California architecture. It's eliminating hallways, taking down walls, and making rooms visually transparent. Furnishing may be the only thing defining the spaces."

Viewed from the street, strong horizontal lines make the homes, inspired by architecture on the Spanish island of Ibiza, feel contemporary. The impression is aided by what looks like a flat roof on one home; it's a deception created by the tall walls that define the open-air front courtyard. Where there is a roof, the pitch is shallow, even by Southern California standards. By employing only two siding materials, stucco and stone, it look as though a large addition were made to a humble main house. Elegantly detailed dark eaves support a simple roof. By limiting adornments to dark wood trellises, custom downspouts, and lanterns, the design focuses attention on the building's pleasing mass. The elevations evidence White's belief that less is more.

Inside, the homes follow a familiar organization. The kitchen, family room, and dining room typically line up along the rear, opening to a back porch and small yard with a pool. Large master bedrooms, typically with dual walk-in closets, a sitting area, and a spacious bathroom, also take their place along the back of the house, where they get the most privacy and best views. Large islands dominate most kitchens—the biggest have two, one for preparing food, the other for eating it. Some designs include prep kitchens, whether for caterers or just to sequester the messy job of cooking to another room. The homes include a wide variety of preplanned options for dens, wine rooms, and garage space for trophy cars. Pantries could be converted to a ventilated room for wok cooking.

When kitchen islands first showed up regularly in the 1990s, it wasn't clear whether they were a keeper. Some seemed simply showy. The worst interfered with work patterns—the vaunted work triangle, which holds that space for food storage, preparation, and cooking needs to be in close proximity. (The triangle has been expanded to a rectangle to include the microwave.) Today, many larger new homes incorporate multiple islands. One may be for preparing food, another for dining, entertaining friends, or doing homework. Islands in luxury homes may be tricked out with everything money can buy—refrigerated wine storage, warming ovens, smartphone recharging centers, brew stations, drawer dishwashers for wine glasses, you name it. "The kitchen is the twenty-first-century living room," White says.

Multi-purpose islands have transformed the kitchen into a hub of family activity. Even in conservative housing markets such as St. Louis and Washington, DC, islands separate kitchens from family rooms in most production homes. Meanwhile, the tradition of eating every meal at the dining room table has given way to movable feasts, a trend that became evident during the 2000s. Research shows that people increasingly consume meals in front of the television, on the back porch, in the basement grotto—wherever it suits them. Food preparation has followed these migratory paths. Witness the many master suites and basement rec rooms that include mini-refrigerators, cabinets, sinks, and coffee klatches.

A kitchen designed for entertaining reads more like a zone within the great room than a dedicated wet room. *Photo courtesy of The New Home Company*

Patio doors open to a poolside loggia, ideal for dining. *Photo courtesy of The New Home Company*

A second home at Coral Crest makes a strong first impression with weathered wood doors, a metal gate, and thick walls that lead to an entry courtyard. *Photo courtesy of The New Home Company*

Larger new homes, including the ones at Coral Crest, include casitas or "bonus" rooms over the garage that function as small apartments. Many include small kitchens, though county ordinances may prohibit builders from including a stove. The spaces are ideal for guests, grown children, and in-laws. They could even be used for rental income. More than one builder now markets homes with dedicated space—sometimes just a basement apartment with a separate entrance—that owners can rent through a shared housing service.

The homes at Coral Crest are built to so-called livability standards. The idea is to design a home that people of all physical abilities can conveniently visit. That basically entails having at least one step-free entry, wider hallways and doorways than you see in most homes, and a first-floor bathroom. That stands in stark contrast to the operating philosophy of builders who purposely sell homes with built-in obsolescence. Just as Ford would like you to trade up from a sporty two-door coup, to a family minivan, and then a luxury four-door sedan, some builders aim to sell you a different home at every stage of your life—first a starter home on the suburban fringe, then a semi-custom home closer to town, and finally a move-down home in a retirement community down the road.

Several homes at Coral Crest include flexible rooms close to bathrooms that could take shape as bedrooms, dens, libraries, wine rooms, in-law suites, or whatever suits your fancy. Who's to say whether your love for fine wine may beget a passion for collecting, or whether you finally make the leap to work at home rather than commute to a corporate office. Maybe you want to plan for the day when ailing parents may need to move in.

A BIG CHALLENGE PRODUCTION BUILDERS FACE is developing homes for close-in suburban rather than exurban locations. To compensate for higher lot prices, they must often go up rather than out, and build homes closer together. That results in many more three-story homes—some with elevators, many with rooftop decks. Careful land planning and home design is essential to make the homes livable, to ensure that neighbors don't have a bird's eye view of your dinner table or the tub in your master bathroom. Providing enough natural light becomes problematic when neighboring homes block the path of sunlight. And it's difficult to provide private outdoor space.

Apex, a neighborhood of tightly spaced detached homes within San Diego's Civita development, successfully addresses each of these issues, which is why it has won numerous industry awards. Perched above a regional shopping center, within an easy commute of downtown, the homes at Apex sit only six feet apart, on lots a mere thirty-eight feet wide by forty-eight feet deep. On lots this narrow, a two-car garage consumes more than half of the home's frontage, leaving very little living space on the first floor for public rooms. The shallowness of the lots creates another big problem. People buying a detached home want a backyard. But creating enough privacy for a hot tub or party space is problematic with another home so close in back.

Architect Mike Woodley decided the best approach would be to design three-story houses with the main living spaces on the second floor. He asks owners to climb a half-flight of stairs to the front door of their 2,000-square-foot house, just like they would in a split-level home from the 1950s. They're rewarded with front doors that open to a spectacular landing suspended in a two-and-a-half-story light cube. Another half-flight up are the family room, dining, and kitchen spaces. A half-flight down is an "activity room." In one model, it's shown as a workout room wrapped with mirrors, a television monitor for twenty-four-hour news, and sleek equipment for lifting weights and doing cardio work. Alternative floor plans show how the space, which includes a full bath, could easily convert into an office or media room, or a private bedroom suite for a boomerang child or elderly parent.

Picture windows rise more than twenty feet on two sides of the entry cube. From the living room on the second floor or study on the third, you can look back through the cube to the storied hills of San Diego. It's like a corner has been cut out of the house. Second-level spaces borrow space from one another, divided only by a fireplace/television wall, with a see-through fireplace option. A small bar, with backlit shelves to show off prized tequila, makes the most of an otherwise dead corner. It sits near the entry to a private balcony, big enough for a small party, yet cozy enough for morning coffee. "That's where you'd grill," says Woodley. "That's where you'd have a cocktail, where you'd see what's happening in the neighborhood. It's a great spot. You are almost looking out over the street."

Moving the public rooms upstairs gave Woodley more room to work with on the first level. He recessed two garages into the building envelope, then cantilevered the balcony over the front of the house to create a partially covered parking space underneath. Homes are set back far enough from the street that the driveways could park two cars. Woodley also found a way to give each home a small, private backyard reached from the activity space. It's big enough to hold a hot tub, grill, or Zen garden, with a little green space left over for the dog to do its thing.

The lessons at Apex: When every square inch is considered, even a 2,000-square-foot house becomes exciting. Each bedroom is designed with a furniture layout in mind, one that provides a private view from the bed and room for furniture along the wall. Plans show how semi-private workspace on the second floor could be enclosed to produce a bedroom with an attached bath. The kitchen island has enough clearance that two people could sit facing each other at breakfast, rather than side by side. The third-floor loft could also be converted into a bedroom. And the laundry room, as is common in many production homes today, follows the bedrooms upstairs, where most dirty clothes are discarded.

The plan moves main living spaces to the upper levels, reserving the first floor for parking and a flexible activity room. *Photo by Jeffrey Aron*

A two-story windowed entry foyer cuts a corner from the box, providing views of the San Diego hillside from three levels. *Photo by Jeffrey Aron*

PLANS: Pre-planned options convert open space to bedrooms and flex space to multiple uses. *Diagram courtesy Woodley Architectural Group*

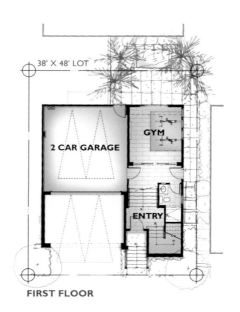

38' X 48' LOT

2 CAR GARAGE

GYM

ENTRY

FIRST FLOOR

PANTRY

PWDR

LIVING

DINING

KITCHEN

OUTDOOR ROOM

OPEN TO BELOW

SECOND FLOOR

BDRM 2

M BATH

OFFICE

MASTER

LAU

OPEN TO BELOW

THIRD FLOOR

GUEST SUITE

GUEST SUITE OPTION AT GYM **FIRST FLOOR**

BONUS ROOM

BONUS ROOM OPTION AT GYM **FIRST FLOOR**

LUXURY BATH

LUXURY BATH OPTION AT MASTER BATH **THIRD FLOOR**

SPA BATH

SPA BATH OPTION AT MASTER BATH **THIRD FLOOR**

SOME OF THE MOST TREND-SETTING PRODUCTION HOUSING IS DONE IN LAS VEGAS, where builders are rewarded for hiring top-drawer architects. Lately, they've been producing modern home designs that stand out from the thousands of Mediterranean-style homes built during the housing boom. Architect Patrick Edinger of edingerArchitects won several industry awards for a series of eclectic homes built at Summerlin, the big masterplanned community west of town. The homes, which ranged in size from 3,000 to 4,000 square feet, sold at an astonishingly rapid pace for around $1.5 million. To contain costs, builder William Lyon Homes sold the houses according to a strict, six-month production schedule. Buyers had two months to make interior finish selections, and no changes were allowed during construction.

With strong horizontal masonry forms, parallel windows, and horizontally stacked cultured stone, the homes looked like no other production housing in Las Vegas. The impression stemmed from an unusually diverse palette of exterior

Strong horizontal lines, man-made materials, and translucent glass highlight these modern production homes in Las Vegas. *Photo courtesy of edingerArchitects*

materials—etched-glass garage doors, frosted glass front doors (some that pivot from a center point), and large horizontal windows broken by unusual brows. Front paths led past small patches of intriguing synthetic cladding, uplit cactus and other desert plants, and rectangular gurgling fountains. Abstract art pieces by the door completed the modern impression.

The interiors featured architectural details typically found only in custom homes—vertical accent walls for televisions and fireplaces, kitchens with lacquered cabinets, natural stone countertops, and brushed metal hardware. Great rooms integrated backlit bars and small wine rooms. Intimate home theater spaces were outfitted with comfortable couches and plush chairs. Galleries in two-story steel-and-glass stairwells often looked back over great rooms. In every case, massive window walls along the back opened the home to spectacular backyards with angular pools, built-in grills and refrigerators, and regimented lawns.

Edinger lifted the best ideas from these homes and used them for ones that sell for half that price on the other side of town. Brookshire Estates sits on the eastern fringe of suburban Las Vegas, an area that suffered from a housing glut during the downturn. The simple, elegant homes keep the horizontal orientation of the luxury homes across town, including the unusual brows that bisect windows and cast horizontal shadows inside. Vertical stone masses break horizontal planes of windows and translucent glass in a contemporary take on prairie style architecture. "Even prairie style architecture, with its emphasis on horizontal lines, typically utilizes vertical window forms," Edinger says.

The homes retain a key interior detail: creative accent walls that hold fireplaces and televisions. They come in a variety of shapes, composed with materials borrowed from the exterior. In one, light-gauge steel cut into plank shapes creates a weathered, rusty appearance. In another, large-format ceramic tile, applied horizontally, imitates a brick pattern. Staggered, stacked-stone veneer frames the fireplace and television in a third model. It's applied tightly, with invisible grout lines to once again emphasize the horizontal plane. The accent walls combine with inspired ceiling designs in key rooms—Edinger boosts roof trusses to leave room underneath to layer ceiling materials. He showed restraint in the master bedroom suites at Brookshire Estates, though they still radiate luxury. Creative media and fireplace walls separate beds from sitting areas. Elaborately zoned bathrooms allocate space to showering, dressing, grooming, and bathing—often in a pearl-shaped tub in the middle of the room. Glass-walled showers are big enough for two, not three.

The production homes make extensive use of off-the-shelf products that used to be custom orders. Traditional building product companies now offer affordably priced products designed to work with contemporary home design. Mainstream plumbing companies market geometric faucets and fixtures. Garage door companies sell doors with translucent glass panes. Fireplace companies make horizontal gas inserts. Interior door companies offer flush doors. Window companies tout contemporary lines with thinner wood profiles and bigger glass panes. Formerly exotic surfaces—cork, concrete, and bamboo flooring—have gone mainstream. The trend works right into the hands of the makers of man-made alternatives to quartz and marble countertops.

13.
RELATE TO URBAN ENVIRONMENTS

The paseo creates a social center for the community. Townhome owners hang out on front stoops large enough for furniture and a grill. Dark planters pick up on the color of metal awnings. The paseos help secure the community in its transitional neighborhood. From the porch or a front window, residents can see who comes and goes. Raising the courtyard four feet provided space for an underground garage with fourteen spaces and bike storage. A detached garage with eighteen spaces serves the remaining homes.

The homes pack a lot of style into three floors of living space. Stairs hug the side to open up living space. White walls, the absence of molding, and dark exotic hardwood floors create a sophisticated look. Small kitchens tricked out with open shelving, backlit glass cabinets, and geometric range hoods reinforce that impression. Bathrooms contain Euro-style

fixtures, slate tile bath surrounds, and colorful floating vanities. The homes divide logically with public rooms on the main floor, bedrooms on the second floor, and an open basement. Some homeowners run a business from the basement. Others use the basements as guest bedrooms or family rooms.

Despite launching sales at the height of the housing recession in mid-2008, the project proved so popular that the developer, Loftworks, managed to raise prices twice and sell out within a year and a half. Sacramento's city manager bought a home. The principal of a major architectural firm purchased another. The project's location—within a block of mass transit and a grocery store, and many of the city's best restaurants—was part of the attraction. With bamboo growing and front stoop plantings in full bloom, the homes look like they've been there for a hundred years. It's no wonder that Sutter Brownstones was the first new-home project featured on the local preservation society's walking tour.

It's East Coast row home meets West Coast modernism at Row Homes on F Street, a Kevin deFreitas design near the Gaslamp district of downtown San Diego. *Photo by Carol Peerce*

Industrial loft details—exposed concrete interior walls, steel I-beams, and open risers—proved a big hit with West Coast buyers. *Photo by Carol Peerce*

Wood floors and cabinets, along with brightly colored furnishings, soften the industrial vibe. *Photo by Carol Peerce*

THE REBIRTH OF URBAN CENTERS HAS GIVEN RISE TO SOME FABULOUS NEW HOUSING ALTERNATIVES. Another celebrated project, Row Homes on F Street, designed by Kevin deFreitas, was built on the leading edge of San Diego's downtown revival in the 2000s. The cluster of seventeen edgy homes, built on spec on an infill lot, blazed an early trail to the city's now vibrant East Village, an eclectic neighborhood of new restaurants, rooftop bars, boutiques, and live music venues. The project hit an urban trifecta. Each three-story home includes a protected stoop, a private roof deck—the urban answer to a backyard—and private parking.

Building homes in a downtown setting is never easy. Stockpiled materials may walk. Traffic makes deliveries a major hassle. To hasten construction and reduce the possibility of theft, the Row Homes crews tilted up massive concrete wall sections to form walls. They had to be exact—just three inches of air space separates the sixteen-and-a-half-foot-wide homes. An alley provides light and ventilation as it hides parking and utilities. Each home includes one garage bay, low by any standards but especially in car-crazy Southern California. But grocery stores, a trolley, and bus stops are all within walking distance.

Tall ceilings and big windows fill the colorful family room with sunlight and fresh air. *Photo by Carol Peerce*

The two-bedroom homes, ranging from 1,500 to 1,850 square feet, accommodate both work and home life. They include flex rooms with street access that can be used as a place of business, accommodating everything from private art galleries to architectural offices. Designed so that they could be easily separated from private areas of the home, the flex rooms could also be used as bedrooms—they'd be great for elderly parents who don't want to climb the stairs or twenty-somethings who want to slip unnoticed into the city at night.

The main public rooms—kitchen, dining, and living, along with a half-bath—share a vaulted second floor. Fourteen-foot-tall aluminum windows fill double-height spaces with daylight and fresh air. The bigger homes have dens. Bedrooms occupy the third floor, where they catch breezes that waft up from the ocean. Each home has a private rooftop deck, an even better place to enjoy the air. Row Homes was one of the first of a new generation of urban projects to include rooftop decks. The housing industry discovered this prized amenity coming out of the downturn, when fears about water leaking through flat roofs ebbed in the face of the need to sell homes. Some builders now market elaborate rooftop "experiences" complete with dining, entertaining, and cooking spaces. You could even sleep outside if you wanted.

Symmetrical massing forms a uniform streetscape that gives Basecamp River North its urban identity. *Photo by Pappageorge Haymes*

Custom kitchens anchor family homes flexible enough to stretch to six bedrooms for multigenerational families. *Photo by Nicholas James*

Each home comes with a rooftop deck, the urban answer to the suburban backyard. *Photo by Nicholas James*

SOME OF THE BEST URBAN HOUSING IS DONE IN CHICAGO, one of the earliest cities to enjoy a renaissance. Basecamp River North in old Irving Point shows how far these undertakings have come. Designed by Pappageorge Haymes Partners, the project combines forty-seven three-story row homes with ten affordable housing units. Each three-story home has a private yard and two-car garage, just like you might get in a masterplanned community outside of town. The homes also share a lushly landscaped community park with room for children and pets, something you may not get in the suburbs. Plus, you are only twenty minutes from downtown, in a neighborhood with landmark architecture, close to a mass transit stop and neighborhood shopping. Who could resist?

Basecamp looks urban because of the repetition of strong forms. But instead of the walk-up porches, bay windows, and turrets you'd see in Hyde Park, these row homes rely on fiber-cement panels and oversized metal-clad windows to create modulated volumes. Extensive use of glass and steel references the city's modern architecture heritage. Basecamp's low-rise scale and the adjacent park contrast pleasantly with the density of high-rise buildings nearby. It creates a refreshing pocket of light and air in the neighborhood. From the street, you'd never know the project includes affordable housing. Integrated between the market-rate homes, the homes maintain the same level of exterior details. They vary only slightly on the interior.

Small front yards connect to paths and a big park, a green oasis within the city. *Photo by Pappageorge Haymes*

SL70's setting—the heterogeneous Silver Lake neighborhood of Central Los Angeles—dictated eclectic home designs. *Photo by Christopher Mayer*

Ten-foot ceilings and open floor plans produce strong entertainment settings. A white interior palette accepts colorful furnishings. *Photo by Christopher Mayer*

Flexible floor plans are even more important in urban housing, which draws a wider variety of buyers and renters. These homes contain from four to six bedrooms with fully finished basements to accommodate the needs of multigenerational households. Circulating fresh air is also a big deal in row homes, especially for units that share walls. Strategically sited bay windows and bump-outs draw air in key spots. Residents who want fresh air can retreat to a landscaped yard wrapped with metal fencing or a private rooftop deck enclosed by low planter walls.

EVEN CITIES SUCH AS LOS ANGELES, WHICH DIDN'T HAVE MUCH OF A DOWNTOWN TO BEGIN WITH, sport pockets of new urban housing. Silver Lake, one of the hippest neighborhoods in Central Los Angeles, filled with boutiques, edgy bars, trend-setting restaurants, and cool music venues, is one of them. The neighborhood draws a creative mix of artists, professionals, and entertainment-industry types. They can jog and walk their dogs in nearby parks. Now, as older buildings come down, they can find edgy new apartment homes.

The seventy new homes at SL70 took the place of a decrepit former Hollywood silent movie studio. Reflective rectangular panels, stacked from the ground to the roof, some brightly colored, mirror the lights and sights of the city. The three-story homes exploit downtown views with great room terraces and rooftop decks. Open floor plans with ten-foot ceilings on the main floor make for easy entertaining, with kitchen, dining, and living zones in one continuous layout. White walls provide a backdrop for colorful furnishings and art. Kitchens—dubbed "culinary retreats" in marketing brochures—include contemporary European style cabinets, large kitchen islands, restaurant-quality appliances, and brushed nickel hardware.

FIRST FLOOR

SECOND FLOOR

THIRD FLOOR

Multiple terraces and rooftop decks make the most of this prized urban location, the former site of a crumbling silent film studio. *Photo by Christopher Mayer*

PLANS / The biggest plan at SL70 includes two master bedrooms, a first-floor office, and a large roof terrace. *Photo by Christopher Mayer*

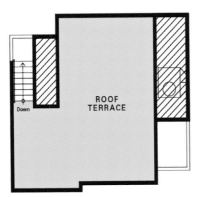

ROOF TERRACE

ROOF TERRACE

Eric Zuziak of JZMK packed a lot of living space within four different floor plans, each less than 1,500 square feet. Side-by-side garages share a first floor with home offices in most plans. Otherwise the designs differ mostly in bedroom arrangements. The idea is to appeal to a broad diversity of potential households, including singles and non-traditional ones. Most homes have two master bedrooms on the second floor, which makes it easy for unrelated, or related couples to share a home. One plan aimed at young families features three bedrooms; two secondary bedrooms share a hall bath.

There's a big debate in development circles over whether Gen Y buyers prefer urban over suburban housing. In the case of SL70, more than two-thirds of the buyers were less than forty years old. The question is whether these households, once they have kids, will move to the suburbs. In the meantime, they can enjoy each other's company. As in the Sutter Brownstone project, front porches connect to paseos that run between rows of homes, providing a social center for the community. Residents who prefer privacy also have the option of retiring to their rooftop deck to soak up the sights and sounds of the city.

14.
WELCOME YOU HOME

FOR MANY PEOPLE, THE COMMUNITY MATTERS MORE THAN THE HOUSE

Tim Busse knows the streets of New Town at St. Charles, in Missouri, like a policeman knows the alleys of Chicago. Only he looks for a different kind of crime. To the town architect of this grand experiment in new suburban living, each home has a special backstory. The principal of H3 Studio points to a de-featured elevation allowed to slip below the community's architectural guidelines during the recession. He grimaces as he notes that the colors of two homes sitting side by side are too much alike; something the town's monotony guidelines strive to avoid. Sometimes he had to swallow hard and approve a design for a cash-

strapped builder eager to make a sale. When Busse allows exceptions to the town's architectural guidelines, he hears about it from the town's self-appointed design police, vocal residents who share in the idealistic vision for this community.

Two goals drive development at New Town at St. Charles: to create a cohesive, architecturally diverse community; and to serve people of all means, not just one income strata, the preferred approach of most developers and their marketing consultants. This grand commitment, combined with the developer's fondness for experimenting with new housing styles—side-by-side homes imported from the Garden District of New Orleans is one example, rural Missouri stacked flats is another—has resulted in one of the most eclectic new-home communities in the nation. Home styles range from row houses along a lane, to apartments in large mansion-like buildings, to one-story starter cottages with white picket fences, to large estate homes fronting a series of man-made lakes and canals.

The "water features" have an interesting story; they resulted from a county requirement to provide eighty acres of storm water retention. Instead of piping storm water into hidden back ponds, the developer decided to make the ponds a defining landmark. Both economic and aesthetic concerns drove the decision. It reduced how much sewer pipe had to be laid. It also meant that most homes could be located close to water—no more than two blocks away. Land at the edge of lakes and canals was left undeveloped and open to the public. Because the community isn't gated, even outsiders show up to swim or fish in the water.

All roads and paths at Pinehills lead
to a village green, the site of concerts, a post office, and a highly
anticipated food truck festival.
Photo courtesy of Pinehills

Pinehills draws its small-town
charm from buildings like the
red-tin-roofed Summerhouse.
Photo courtesy of Pinehills

Over lunch at the colonial-era Rye Tavern, Green explains that he organized small neighborhoods to conserve open space, trees, and wildlife habitat. He mapped out homes to harmonize with woodland, pond, and golf course settings, often with rear great rooms that face nature. A byzantine network of walking and biking trails connects the neighborhoods to shops, cafès, a bank, the post office, and the Village Green, the centerpiece of the community and home to innumerable cultural and social events. Residents can go on long walks through the woods for exercise. Or they can engage in a variety of active sports—golf, kayaking, swimming, tennis, and weightlifting.

An endless variety of housing types—affordable apartments, stylish townhomes, one-story villas, storybook cottages, spacious portfolio homes, and one-of-a-kind custom homes—means that nearly anyone could find a home here. Homes in some neighborhoods are restricted to buyers fifty-five or older. Green even brought in a provider of assisted living, which is rarely done in new home communities—developers don't want buyers thinking about "next steps." In the meantime, Pinehills residents gain access to more than thirty clubs at the Stonebridge Club, and two championship golf courses. Roughly 3,000 people will eventually call the community home.

At the Village Green, a traditional social and commercial center like you find in old New England villages, you can have your hair done, mail a package, find a unique gift, meet a friend for coffee, do your grocery shopping, have your car serviced, and pick up a bottle of wine for dinner. The center lays claim to more than twenty-five shops and services and 1.3 million square feet of commercial office space. Bands perform concerts throughout the summer.

Smart planning breaks down the Pinehills into comfortable, picturesque neighborhoods. Varied front yards, lots at odd angles, and variations in building massing make it look like streets were built one house at a time. When the same floor plans were built along streets to achieve production economies, garages, bump-outs, and color palettes were varied to avoid monotony. It's tough to tell the homes are alike until you step inside and see a familiar room arrangement or fireplace detail.

NEW ENGLAND HAS A LONG HISTORY OF COTTAGE COMMUNITIES THAT SHARE GARDENS, pools, and small community buildings. The communal spaces—which may come at the expense of smaller yards—create a sense of belonging that's missing in larger planned communities. Architect Doug Kallfelz of Union Studio in Providence, Rhode Island, studied many of these older cottage villages before he designed Heritage Sands on Cape Cod, overlooking Nantucket Sound. Families used to make annual pilgrimages to these summer communities to enjoy time at the beach and try to forget about work back home.

Kallfelz found that many of the old enclaves began as tent sites for working-class families—teachers, policeman. Then simple wood-framed cottages were built, in many cases by the residents themselves. The homes were often basic, since the residents weren't people of great means and the emphasis was on enjoying the sea and the company of other families. "Many people emulated details from classic homes, only they used economical materials," he says.

Kallfelz also drew inspiration from the Federal Housing Administration's infamous 1940 guidance for small houses. The agency, concerned about providing enough affordable homes for returning veterans, advised designers and builders to cut costs by avoiding unnecessary gable and dormers, breaks in the roof, and over-elaborate cornices. Instead, it recommended that they concentrate on scale and careful placement of windows and doors. Make houses look larger, and easier to build, the FHA said, by using one siding material. The only additions the agency recommended were porches, bay windows, and platform steps. "Sometimes people forget that the best neighborhoods, the ones we cherish, are made of great solid principles of form, scale, and simple craftsman detailing, the kind that architects used to do," Kallfelz says. "They can be elegant and beautiful, and still simple."

For Heritage Sands, located on the site of a former RV park, Kallfelz relied on simple gabled Cape Cods with one to three bedrooms and a maximum of 1,350 square feet in living space. Dining, living, and kitchen areas draw visual space from each other in open floor plans. Tall (nine-foot) first-floor ceilings, the occasional vault, and generous glass make the homes feel roomy, as do back patios that are critical to grilling, drinking, and spending quality vacation time. Each cottage enjoys at least a sliver of an ocean view, some from wrap-around porches, thanks to green space that extends deep into the community.

There's plenty to do at Heritage Sands. Homeowners share access to a clubhouse with an exercise room and a pool big enough for families to square off in water volleyball. A catering kitchen and clubhouse lounge facilitate community gatherings. Crushed shell paths wind down to a private beach with a launch and fishing jetties. Pavilions along the path provide perches to enjoy ocean views and wafts. Because the community lies within the Cape's seasonal resort district, families may only use the homes from April through October—and four days per month during the winter.

Kallfelz kept the design of windows, doors, and rooflines simple. He drew most walls, floors, and ceilings in four- or eight-foot dimensions, the standard width and length of lumber, plywood, and drywall used in construction. The homes were built from modules assembled in a factory, which helped with quality control and meeting modern-day requirements for energy efficiency and hurricane resistance. The frame was packed with extra insulation and checked for air gaps before it left the factory. Steel straps tie the homes to their foundations. Windows can withstand hurricane-force winds.

The homes at Heritage Sands wear modest gray cedar shingle siding, with simple window patterns, doors, and rooflines. White trim wraps windows, doors, porches—even the house itself. The only seeming extravagances: wrap-under gable ends and colorful front doors in pink, blue, and red. "Even people with means on the Cape prefer an understated, practical architecture that defers to the community by not drawing attention to itself," Kallfelz says. "The traditional cottage communities tend to avoid being too precious, focusing more on the quality of the community experience."

ARCHITECT ROSS CHAPIN HAS HELPED ENGINEER THE COMEBACK OF COTTAGE COMMUNITIES ON THE OPPOSITE COAST—in the Pacific Northwest. While Chapin's communities have a nostalgic appeal—it's hard to resist their community gardens, white picket fences, and charming dwellings—he doesn't consider his architecture traditional. If anything, the details are more contemporary, with straight, simple lines. "Their form follows their function," says Chapin. "The purists of traditional architecture are doing things that are not of our time. They are working with materials, craftsmanship, and labor that relate to another period."

Chapin is more concerned with the here and now. He was deeply influenced by an immensely practical builder he worked for in one of his first jobs out of architectural school. When faced with a design or construction challenge, the

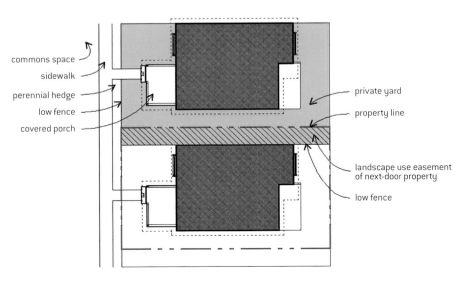

commons space
sidewalk
perennial hedge
low fence
covered porch

private yard
property line

landscape use easement
of next-door property

low fence

recycling them from previous projects—before he bought new ones. He'd take time to properly install and weatherproof siding, windows, and roofing so that he wouldn't have to repeat his work in a few years. He'd pay close attention to how the building functions—whether stale air was vented from stables, whether barns were safe from fire, whether moisture could get into grain bins.

Chapin subjects his designs to similar tests. He keeps extra details to a minimum. He sources as much material locally as possible. "Good architecture may or may not cost more," he says. "I prefer to concern myself with questions like what materials can you get locally and inexpensively from Home Depot, rather than sourcing refined quartz from other parts of the world or cutting wood from an old-growth forest. We've done a lot of good work with inexpensive vinyl tile and laminates."

Chapin draws inspiration from Christopher Alexander's pattern language, particularly the idea that a web of relationships creates a sense of place. He thinks about how the community center relates to its edges. How porches relate to common green space. How the roofs and eaves convey a sense of shelter. And especially how to create a sense of arrival. "That can be influenced by the transition from car to the door as we enter the house," he says. "Is the path straight or curved? Is there a place to sit next to the door and take off your boots? Is it covered? How would you describe the feel of the building at that point? Does it feel substantial? Is it thick in a way that helps reinforce the larger community patterns?"

At Spring Valley, a pocket neighborhood of ten cottages Chapin designed in Port Townsend, Washington, the "coming home" experience starts with parking a car on the perimeter in an assigned space. Residents then walk down paths that border shared green space, gardens, and a commons building. As they get deeper into the community, homes step back to create a more expansive open space. Low picket fences between the cottages—they range from 600 to 1,200 square feet and sold originally for less than $200,000—serve mostly to mark flowerbeds and front yards. Front walks lead to a short flight of steps up to a front porch generous enough to hold a porch swing, table, and chairs. Planters hang from porch railings, making the homes seem like an extension of their gardens.

A simple exterior palette—board and batten siding with white trim—belies sophisticated floor plans. Dining alcoves, with windows on three sides, look out on the green space. So do bay windows with built-in seating, drawers underneath to store pillows, and shelves on either side to hold books. Dutch doors on some homes permit spring fragrances to enter but prevent pets from exiting. The open cottage plans often include an "away" room—an office or den where household members can go to work, read, or just escape.

Chapin consciously orients active living spaces (kitchen, dining, and living) toward the shared commons and positions private spaces toward the back of the house and upstairs. Each cottage has an open side with windows facing a side yard and a closed side with high, private windows. Actual property lines are located at least five feet from the closed side of the house, per building codes. But easements allow owners to enjoy the full use of the side yard on the open side up to the closed face of their neighbor's house. It's those small details that make Chapin's communities so livable and celebrated. "Privacy and layering of personal space are critically important to the social health of a community," he says.

15.
RISE TO THE LEVEL OF ART

BEAUTY MAY BE THE ULTIMATE TEST OF SUSTAINABILITY

The stepped boardwalk that transports visitors to Hog Pen Creek in Austin, Texas, certainly evokes a strong sense of place. It leads to a home on the shores of Lake Austin that in many ways is the ultimate lake house. First stop is a relaxing, two-story outdoor living room with a large concrete fireplace wall, steel beams, and comfortable wood armchairs. Once inside, lift and slide doors open the house to lake breezes. Mysterious catwalks overhead lead to rooms enclosed with glass to provide lake views. The boardwalk culminates in a lakeside dining pavilion that looks like the end of a pier.

After Hog Pen Creek received one of architecture's highest honors—a Housing Award from the American Institute of Architects—images of the iconic house graced the association's website for a year. Designed by Brian Comeaux of Lake|Flato, the home is far more than the sum of its wonderful cedar, stone, and steel parts. In fact, some might say it rises to the level of art, especially after close inspection. Comeaux wrapped the kitchen and master bedroom with red cedar siding to create a home within the home. And he gave the home a shed roof that subtly mimics the slope of the land.

But what does the public think? Comeaux put the home to that all-important test one late summer weekend when he opened it to visitors. The weather cooperated. Cool breezes wafted up from the lake, cooling the house through the open walls of doors. Occasionally, for effect, Comeaux would close a massive, sixteen-foot barn door to the master bedroom designed to block morning sun. The noise startled tour-goers. "It makes a low rumbling sound, like a train coming down the tracks," he says.

Otherwise, visitors seemed preoccupied with details that Comeaux takes for granted. "They would walk into the kitchen and ask, 'Where's the refrigerator?' Of course, we hid the appliances behind paneling. That's something that we do all the time on our houses," he says. "But most people hadn't seen it before." Tour-goers were also curious about the wood on the kitchen floor. "It's end-grain mesquite, cut into four-by-six-inch blocks and laid out in a random staggered pattern. We stain it black, but it has a reddish appearance. It looks really nice."

The detail that raised the most eyebrows, though, was a metal grate that rolls to cover either the fireplace or the television. "It playfully forces a choice," says Comeaux. "You can enjoy the ambiance of a fire, but you can't watch TV. Or you can watch TV, but you can't have a fire. The great thing about working on this project was that one of the clients was a graphic artist. They gave me the creative freedom to run with my ideas."

The house, with only 2,836 square feet of conditioned living space, looks much bigger than that from the street. The system of external boardwalks and catwalks reduced the need for space-consuming internal hallways. Large porches also reduced the need for interior space. During insect season, the

An elevated boardwalk welcomes visitors to Hog Pen Creek. A metal roof with broad overhangs references hill country architecture. *Photo by Casey Dunn*

Take your pick—a panel slides to reveal either the fireplace or TV, but not both. *Photo by Casey Dunn*

A concrete lap pool, with a wall that supports the house, provides a third "water" view from key indoor spots. *Photo by Casey Dunn*

Two porches—one open, one screened—extend the outdoor living season at Hog Pen Creek. *Photo by Casey Dunn*

End-grain mesquite kitchen flooring and hidden appliances surprised visitors on an architectural tour. *Photo by Casey Dunn*

owners—a San Francisco couple who wanted a vacation home in Texas, where they grew up—retreat to a two-story screened porch on the north side. It's an ideal perch from which to enjoy the majestic pecan, oak, and cypress trees preserved on the site. Only one tree was lost during construction—a pecan uprooted during a storm. It was recycled into a dining room table, vanity tops, and shelves.

The owners had a relatively short design agenda. They wanted to take advantage of lake views on the five-acre property. They wanted two offices, since they both work. And they wanted a seventy-five-foot lap pool for triathlon training. Comeaux was surprised to learn that easements, flood plain restrictions, and building setbacks reduced the buildable area considerably. "They had all this land, but because of all the restrictions they could only build on a quarter acre," he says. "And there was a heritage oak in the middle of it."

Comeaux designed an L-shaped home, built primarily with steel and filled in with Douglas fir members. Two wings form a courtyard around the live oak, which was hit by lightning during construction but nursed back to health. The best lake views were reserved for the two-story main wing containing the kitchen, living and dining spaces, and master suite. A three-story entry separates the main wing from the one-story west wing, which houses a carport and two guest

An entry walk that bisects the wings
of the Beaux Arts House points
toward the biggest tree on the lot.
*Photo courtesy Cutler Anderson
Architects*

bedrooms—one for yoga, the other for music. Murphy beds drop from the wall to convert the spaces into guest rooms, another detail that intrigued tour-goers.

Comeaux decided the best place for the lap pool was along the west side of the house, away from the lake. That way the main house could have "water" views on three sides—the pool to the west, Hog Pen Creek to the north, and Lake Austin to the east. One side of the pool, built with board-formed concrete, actually supports the house. The pool is elevated three feet above the finished floor of the main house, at waist level with someone inside the house. A long strip window provides views of swimmers as they pass by.

A piano is all that divides living from dining areas in the great room. Off to one side, a seating area with built-in bookshelves and a fireplace provides a getaway space. A small office, adjacent to a hall bathroom that serves as the first-floor powder room, could be converted to a bedroom. A second office sits like a glazed "crow's nest" above the outdoor living room. It's accessed either by an outdoor stair that sneaks up behind the outdoor fireplace or an external catwalk that connects to the second-floor master suite.

Hog Pen Creek is linked to the water in more ways than one. Pipes run under the house and out to the lake in a closed-loop geothermal system that heats and cools the house and pool. The system also preheats domestic water. Surrounding trees work with broad roof overhangs to reduce heat gain during the summer. Water to irrigate the lawn also comes from the lake rather than the city's potable water supply.

When Comeaux started the project, he thought he was designing a "second home with a future." He included an elaborate, remotely controlled home automation system that turns on or off virtually every system in the house. From their home in San Francisco, the owners could even go online to view the home's electrical consumption on a circuit-by-circuit basis in real time, as well as data on temperature, humidity, and CO_2 levels. However, the couple liked the house so much they quickly made it their primary residence.

THE DEFINING FEATURE OF ARCHITECT JIM CUTLER'S BEAUX ARTS HOUSE MAY NOT EVEN BE THE HOUSE. The home and its three courtyards seem to exist mostly to wrap seven mature Douglas fir trees. Designed for a family of six on a grassy lot in a quiet Bellevue, Washington, suburb, the home and its humble palette of brick, wood, and steel is barely visible from the street. Cutler oriented the rooms, doors, and windows so that each major sight line ends with a framed view of a tree. He reserved the biggest piece of glass, eight feet by thirteen feet, for the biggest tree. The magnificent specimen comes into view from the path to the front door. "It's not a look-at-me building," says Cutler. "It's quiet and connected to the living world."

The home belongs to a couple with four children who had spent the previous fourteen years in China. All the time spent in an urban environment heightened their craving for natural beauty. At one time they even fantasized about living in a tree house. Ironically, that may be the best description of what Cutler gave them. Trees wind so tightly around the home that an arborist worked on-site nearly full time during construction to ensure their survival. If the home emphasizes the tree-loving culture of the Pacific Northwest, it also reminds the owners of a traditional courtyard home where they lived in Shanghai.

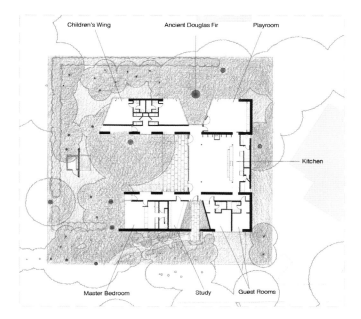

Children's Wing   Ancient Douglas Fir   Playroom

Kitchen

Master Bedroom   Study   Guest Rooms

PLANS / Cutler designed the home to
ensure lines of sight to mature trees
and provide plenty of space for
children to play. *Photo courtesy
Cutler Anderson Architects*

The Beaux Arts House may not be as much fun as living in a tree house, but it's certainly a great home for children. Cutler left room for each child to keep a desk for schoolwork in a large "playroom." There's also enough floor space to comfortably build a block fort, do a puzzle, or play Twister. Activities can be supervised from the kitchen, which is on a diagonal line of sight with the playroom. The playroom door can be closed if it gets too noisy inside or children need to concentrate on their homework.

Cutler's floor plan expediently divides the home into two wings—one for children, the other for grown-ups. Two kids' bedrooms and the playroom occupy one side; the master bedroom, a study, and two guest rooms make up the other. Floor to ceiling glass connects the bedrooms to the courtyard. With the blinds open and the trees lit up, the feeling is a lot like sleeping in the woods.

The wings meet in a tall-ceilinged central gathering space wrapped with wood on all four sides. Four steel columns, softened with wood inserts, support the wood roof. A wall of weight-balanced, glazed vertical lift doors opens the gathering room to a south-facing courtyard. Indoor beams visually connect to outdoor rafters that support an eight-foot cantilever over the smooth back patio, a nice place to enjoy an evening cocktail or ride a Hot Wheel bike. At the far end of the lawn, a brick wall provides the backdrop for a built-in hot tub that could be mistaken for a pond in the grass.

A kitchen, with appliances hidden behind cabinetry fronts, anchors the gathering room. From behind a large built-in island, cooks can look tranquilly through the house to the patio and courtyard. Area rugs mark activity zones within the gathering room. Pianists can practice or entertain to one side. Loungers can curl up in front of a fireplace on the other. Readers can pull a book from a bookcase module. Low drawers bring storage for games and toys within reach of the smallest children.

The Mohican Hills House draws inspiration for its form from nearby split-level homes. *Photo by Anice Hoachlander*

The Mohican Hills House draws inspiration for its form from nearby split-level homes. *Photo by Anice Hoachlander*

The modern interpretation of a woodstove warms a master bedroom that appears perched in the trees. *Photo by Anice Hoachlander*

The arrival sequence is carefully choreographed for maximum impact. Guests travel a meandering path that eventually arrives at two brick pillars marking the main entry path; it bisects the wings and leads deep into the house. The path focuses attention on the big Douglas fir, visible through a glass front door that opens into a corner of the great room. The vertical lift doors and large courtyard don't come into view until you've entered the house.

Cutler relied on visual techniques to lighten what might otherwise seem like a heavy building. Brick used to build the wings makes the steel-framed gathering space seem lighter by comparison. The roof appears to float thanks to clerestory windows and exposed roof supports in the gathering space. Glass bolted over the face of the brick, a technique Cutler borrowed from the Swedish architect Sigurd Lewerentz, lightens the mass of the walls. "Many architects ignore simple tools," says Cutler. "If you want something to feel light, contrast it with something heavy. If you want it to feel bright, contrast it with something dark."

ARCHITECT ROBERT GURNEY SHARES CUTLER'S FASCINATION WITH THE WAY HOMES GO TOGETHER. His early experience working alongside his father, a bricklayer, left him with a deep appreciation for materials—and their possibilities. Early in his career, he built the homes he designed. Today, he uses his building expertise to design challenging modern homes that have won international design awards. In his Mohican Hills House in a neighborhood of Maryland, L-shaped masses fit together almost like blocks, with logical support from below. Rows of windows pick up on the linear form of the boxes. The design seems to playfully update mid-century homes in the neighborhood. "Maybe it does in the end, but that was not intended," Gurney says.

The architect was more interested in taking advantage of views from the top of the ridge. An inward-focused existing home was leveled to the foundation to make way for the new one. The program was simple. "The clients wanted a light-filled house that opened to a lawn and took advantage of the winter views toward the river," says Gurney. The new home integrates high-ceiling volumes with intimate spaces. A three-story, light-filled foyer greets visitors. Globes (*Moooi Random*, designed by Bertjan Pot) orbit the foyer. A glass railing in the second-story loft preserves views to an outdoor clearing, occupied by a lone firepit.

With so many windows, heating and cooling could be problematic. But coated (low-e) windows prevent too much heat from escaping during the winter and too much light entering in the summer. Solar-sensitive shades close automatically when room temperatures reach a threshold. During the winter, the darkly stained concrete slab on the main floor stores solar heat for use at night. Otherwise, energy-saving appliances, light fixtures, and HVAC equipment make miserly use of fossil fuels.

The house is organized around a two-story great room that masterfully integrates the various spaces, each with carefully considered views. A piano, with a view that could inspire some Debussy, separates living and dining spaces. Around the corner, a wall of bookshelves, a fireplace, and a table with two chairs define a minimalist library. A small first-floor office could be converted to a fifth bedroom. The ceiling drops to form a sleek, angular kitchen. Long slabs of half-inch synthetic Silestone, used to form a countertop and table, reinforce the home's horizontal orientation.

A long kitchen countertop slab reinforces the home's horizontal orientation. *Photo by Anice Hoachlander*

A side view reveals a rain screen and protected porches that wrap the house. *Photo by Anice Hoachlander*

A book wall and fireplace form a minimalist library that could be converted into a bedroom. *Photo by Anice Hoachlander*

Precise, clean interiors result from advance consideration of lighting, storage, and furniture needs. Recessed lighting removes the clutter of floor and table lamps. Built-in storage reduces furniture needs. Switches, fireplace grates, and cabinet hardware work in design harmony. Exterior materials find their way inside. Fiber-cement panels, for example, form a tall TV wall in the living room and a bedroom fireplace. With its whimsical cylindrical vent, the fireplace resembles a minimalist version of a wood stove. Together with windows that look to the trees, it makes the master live like a cabin in the woods.

What looks to be the rear wall of the house is actually a rain screen that hides covered porches accessed from most rooms on the first and second floors. A side view reveals where the horizontal and vertical sections intersect, one supporting the other. Some of the porches, contrary to first impressions, actually cantilever over the side of the building—a prime example of how Gurney's knowledge of how buildings go together elevates their design.

ANOTHER EXAMPLE OF A HOME THAT REACHES THE REALM OF ART IS JOHNSEN SCHMALING'S PLEATED HOUSE. It nearly disappears into the woods on a narrow peninsula near Lake Michigan. Charred wood siding installed over furring strips of various sizes echoes the depth and texture of bark. The siding pattern forms an undulating, curtain-like building skin. "It creates an almost ambiguous boundary with the woods instead of a smooth, clearly defined exterior wall," Schmaling says. A green roof, topped with slow-growing sedum that mirrors the color of the tree canopy, aides in the perception. Dark, recessed aluminum windows fade into the background.

The rough texture of the exterior walls contrasts with the smooth finish of the home's forecourt, a wall of milled lumber stacked at slight angles and finished with a lustrous varnish. Since visitors pass the home's rough exterior to enter the smooth forecourt, it's as though they are entering a sawn tree, its smooth side finished like it would be for a coffee table. The tapering forecourt focuses attention on a glazed entry vestibule that frames a view of deep woods on the opposite side of the house.

Dark cedar siding and a green roof make the Pleated House almost disappear into the Michigan woods. *Photo by John J. Macaulay/Johnsen Schmaling Architects*

The vestibule connects to open living space with sliding glass doors that take up the entire back wall. They lead out to a long patio, slightly sunken and contained by an illuminated concrete bench. Inside the house, low ceilings, white walls, and a polished gray concrete floor keep the focus on exterior views. One exception: a sculptural steel staircase, supported from above by a latticework of vertical rods. It anchors the living space and leads to a bedroom suite with access to the green roof. The house contains only two bedrooms. A first-floor graphic design studio, separated from the great room by a sliding door, flexes to a bedroom when guests visit.

Milled lumber, varnished and
stacked at a slight angle, forms an
enticing forecourt that cuts deep
into the building mass. *Photo by
John J. Macaulay/Johnsen
Schmaling Architects*

Spare interiors focus attention on
art objects and surrounding woods.
*Photo by John J. Macaulay/Johnsen
Schmaling Architects*

A green roof with slow-growing sedum
can be accessed from the master
bedroom. *Photo by John J. Macaulay/
Johnsen Schmaling Architects*

The 1,850-square-foot home, designed for empty nesters approaching retirement, makes the most of a gently sloping four-acre site. It's cooled during the summer by breezes from Lake Michigan. Heat comes from a ground source heat pump; fluid runs through piping drilled vertically 250 feet into the ground. Closed-cell, bio-based foam insulates the walls and ceiling. A rain garden reduces consumption of potable utility water. The home was built for about $281 a square foot, which works out to about $520,000, excluding land. Exterior landscaping and the patio added another $50,000.

The Pleated House demonstrates that great design can be within financial reach. Which is a good thing. Now that home values have recovered and homes feel like a safe investment again, the American love affair with them has been rekindled. Homeowners are painting walls, adding the family room addition they always wanted, putting on a deck, or installing the latest app-controlled home system. Increasingly, they are taking the ultimate plunge—working with an architect and builder to design the home of their dreams. Maybe it's a super-green house in the woods, like the Pleated House. Maybe it's a suburban home with a big backyard where they can play catch with a budding baseball star.

In each case, it's important not to lose sight of the ultimate goal: creating a more enriching lifestyle. And that can be achieved in many ways—some simple, some expensive. It's the thought that counts. When I broached the subject of what constitutes a great home at dinner one night, a friend told me emphatically that every home her family had lived in was a great home. She and her husband had worked hard to make it that way. Never mind that it hadn't won an architectural design award.

A BOHEME DESIGN
Rosemary Beach, Florida
abohemedesign.com

ANGELENO ASSOCIATES
Santa Anna, California
angelenoarchitects.com

ARCHIMANIA
Memphis, Tennessee
archimania.com

BAR ARCHITECTS
San Francisco, California
bararch.com

BARLEY | PFEIFFER ARCHITECTURE
Austin, Texas
barleypfeiffer.com

CENTERBROOK ARCHITECTS AND PLANNERS
Essex, Connecticut
centerbrook.com

CUTLER ANDERSON ARCHITECTS
Bainbridge Island, Washington
cutler-anderson.com

EDINGERARCHITECTS
Solano Beach, California
edingerarchitects.com

ESTES TWOMBLY ARCHITECTS
Newport, Rhode Island
estestwombly.com

FOREST STUDIO
Laguna Beach, California
foreststudio.com

H3 STUDIO
St. Louis, Missouri
h3studio.com

HOUSE + HOUSE ARCHITECTS
San Francisco, California
houseandhouse.com

JEFFREY BERKUS ARCHITECTS
Aspen, Colorado
berkusdesign.com

JOHNSEN SCHMALING ARCHITECTS
Milwaukee, Wisconsin
johnsenschmaling.com

JZMK PARTNERS
Costa Mesa, California
jzmkpartners.com

KEVIN DEFREITAS ARCHITECTS
San Diego, California
defreitasarchitects.com

KHOURY VOGT
Seacrest, Florida
khouryvogt.com

KIPNIS ARCHITECTURE + PLANNING
Chicago, Illinois
kipnisarch.com

LAKE | FLATO
San Antonio, Texas
lakeflato.com

LANDER GROUP
Minneapolis, Minnesota
landergroup.com

LOONEY RICKS KISS
Memphis, Tennessee
lrk.com

LPAS
Sacramento, California
lpas.com

MCINTURFF ARCHITECTS
Bethesda, Maryland
mcinturffarchitects.com

MUSE ARCHITECTS
Bethesda, Maryland
musearchitects.com

OBIE G. BOWMAN ARCHITECT
Healdsburg, California
obiebowman.com

PAPPAGEORGE HAYMES PARTNERS
Chicago, Illinois
pappageorgehaymes.com

RICHARD WILLIAMS ARCHITECTS
Washington, DC
richardwilliamsarchitects.com

ROBERT GURNEY ARCHITECT
Washington, DC
robertgurneyarchitect.com

ROSS CHAPIN ARCHITECTS
Langley, Washington
rosschapin.com

UNION STUDIO
Providence, Rhode Island
unionstudioarch.com

WOODLEY ARCHITECTURAL GROUP
Littleton, Colorado
woodleyarchitecture.com

ZACK | DE VITO ARCHITECTURE + CONSTRUCTION
San Francisco, California
zackdevito.com

Copyright © 2018 by Boyce Thompson
Library of Congress Control Number: 2017951876

Designed by Danielle D. Farmer & Cover design by Molly Sheilds
Front cover: Photo by Tom Arban

Back cover: Photos by Zack | de Vito Architecture and Bruce Damonte (top), Tom Arban (middle), and Darren Bradley (bottom)

Type set in Jaapokki/Conduit ITC
ISBN: 978-0-7643-5465-6, Printed in China

Published by Schiffer Publishing, Ltd.
4880 Lower Valley Road, Atglen, PA 19310
Phone: (610) 593-1777; Fax: (610) 593-2002
E-mail: Info@schifferbooks.com, Web: www.schifferbooks.com

For our complete selection of fine books on this and related subjects, please visit our website at www.schifferbooks.com. You may also write for a free catalog.

Schiffer Publishing's titles are available at special discounts for bulk purchases for sales promotions or premiums. Special editions, including personalized covers, corporate imprints, and excerpts, can be created in large quantities for special needs. For more information, contact the publisher.

We are always looking for people to write books on new and related subjects. If you have an idea for a book, please contact us at proposals@schifferbooks.com.

Other Schiffer Books on Related Subjects:

Contemporary Texas Architecture, E. Ashley Rooney, with Joseph Adams, Kevin Alter, and Craig McMahon, ISBN 978-0-7643-5238-6

Contemporary Home Design, Wolfgang Bachmann & Arno Lederer,
ISBN 978-0-7643-4847-1

Architecture Tours L.A. Guidebook: Downtown, Laura Massino Smith,
ISBN 978-0-7643-2084-2